Another Brown Bag

Another Brown Bag

(filled with sermons for children)

by

Jerry Marshall Jordan
Illustrated by Mary Lou Anderson

The Pilgrim Press
New York

Library of Congress Cataloging in Publication Data

Jordan, Jerry Marshall, 1937-
    Another brown bag.

    1. Children's sermons. I. Title.
BV4315.J67   252'.53   80-36849
ISBN 0-8298-0406-4 (pbk.)

Biblical quotations are from the *Revised Standard Version of the Bible,* copyright
1946, 1952 and ©1971 by the Division of Christian Education, National Council
of Churches and are used by permission. Orange Crush ® is a registered
trademark of Crush International Inc. (see sermon No. 3). The two lines from
"I'm Forever Blowing Bubbles" on page 96 are © 1919 Warner Bros. Inc.,
Copyright Renewed, All Rights Reserved. Used by permission. The "Dennis the
Menace" cartoon of October 12, 1978, on page 117, is used by permission of
Hank Ketcham and copyright by Field Enterprises Inc.

The Pilgrim Press, 132 West 31 Street, New York, New York 10001

To my father and mother

Contents

Preface

Since *The Brown Bag*—my first book of sermons for children—was published, I have received many requests for another bagful. Here is *Another Brown Bag*. But before we open this bagful, I want to share a few thoughts with you.

Each Sunday is highlighted by many eager children sitting with me on the chancel steps. Because they are so receptive (which underscores the importance of the time I spend with the children!), I am inspired to prepare these sermons carefully. If the vocabulary is too advanced, the sentences too complex, the thoughts too disconnected, the style too indirect, the time too long, the illustrations too remote, or the moral too obtuse, then I've more work to do!

Children must become involved and participate in the sermons prepared for them. If not, time has been wasted. I encourage their comments, often asking open-ended questions, and I welcome their replies. The more they are involved, the better. Whenever they want to contribute, I try to incorporate what they say into the flow of thought that is being established.

I keep this time with the children positive. I'm careful to avoid put-downs or reprimands that would have a negative and counterproductive result.

The style I use is often autobiographical. Most of the sermons in this collection are of this kind. As a result, the stamp of my personal experience is obvious. I use this style primarily because it is more intimate and direct. Whenever a person says to another, "Let me tell you what happened to me," there is usually a ready listener. Certainly one must be careful in using this style to avoid the pitfall of saying in an egotistical way, "Look what I've done!" Instead, I have tried to keep in mind the Christian message I want to relate through my experiences. Another advantage of this style is that it takes what is often said in the remoteness of the third person into the excitement of the first person. I hope this will inspire others to draw from their own personal experiences and incorporate them into their sermons for children.

I want to express appreciation to the artist, Mary Lou Anderson, for the fine work she has done in drawing the props I've used, and to my two readers, Dr. P. Roy Brammell and Jean Peterson, who have given me some valuable suggestions in the preparation of these sermons for publication. And in particular I want to thank Gayle and our two children, Tap and Suzanne, for their encouragement and help.

It has been my joy to share these sermons with the children of the First Congregational Church (United Church of Christ), Colorado Springs, Colorado.

And now on with another bagful.

No. 1

Curious?

How curious are you? Do you like to know about things? Do you ask questions? A lot of questions? Are you curious, curious, curious?

Some of you are, I know, because you're trying to peek into my brown bag, trying to see what I've brought this morning. That's OK.

May I introduce you to my friend? Curious George. You may already know George. In fact, you may have your own curious friend at home. My son has had this one for years. As a result, this Curious is a little worse for wear. You've read, I'm sure, or have had read to you, the books about Curious George. Fun reading, right?

There's something I like about this George. He wanted to know about everything. So do I. Of course, that's impossible. There's just too much to know in this big world of ours, and there's too little time to learn it all.

But we can learn more—every day! That's why it's important to be curious. You can't learn without being curious, without questioning what things are all about.

Surely this is how God wants us to be. Why else would God have given us a mind? With our five senses (taste, touch, sight, smell, and hearing) we can take it all in. I think God is sad if we don't do this, if we're not curious. So let's ask those questions that need to be asked, and then let's do our best to get the right answers.

But there is something to remember about all this curiosity, something our little friend didn't pay any attention to and that was the cause of all his troubles. While he was being curious, he didn't use his head. You see, he didn't ask how his actions were affecting others. As a result, he made a "monkey" of himself.

What we need to do, as we learn more and more about life, is know what the right and wrong things are to do and how what we do helps or hurts others. That means being curious in a "good" sense.

So, I say to you: Be curious. Go ahead and ask all the questions you can. Read books. Talk with others. Look, listen, and learn. Keep your mind working. Be curious, curious, curious. But be curious in the right way. Don't make a "monkey" of yourself like our little friend did.

Oh, Curious George, we love you. But we could tell you something about being curious, something we will remember—that we shouldn't let our curiosity get us into trouble.

Let us pray.
Dear God: Make us more curious about your wonderful world and about how we may use what we learn for the good of others. Amen.

No. 2

For Best Results

How many of you brushed your teeth this morning? Well, of course, all of you did. What a silly question that is for me to ask.

But let me ask you another question about your tooth-brushing habits. When you squeeze the toothpaste out of the tube, do you squeeze from the top of the tube or from the bottom? I see. Some of you do it from the top and some from the bottom. Which is the right way?

Surely you know that there is a right way. At least on the tube of toothpaste my family uses, the correct way is printed on the back in large letters. Here, let me show you: "FOR BEST RESULTS, SQUEEZE TUBE FROM THE BOTTOM AND FLATTEN IT AS YOU GO UP." I'm afraid I do it wrong. I squeeze from the top. I understand why it should be squeezed from the bottom, but I've always squeezed it from the top, and it seems to me that it doesn't much matter whether you squeeze it from the top or the bottom, so I just continue to be a top-squeezing man.

What are you going to do with me? Put me in jail, or just overlook how I squeeze my toothpaste? You may not like the way I do it, but you are very kind to me, and you feel it's really not important enough to make a fuss over.

That's the way I feel about it too. It's not

important enough to make a fuss over.

You know, the same is true in a lot of other ways. For example, a boy may wear funny-looking clothes or clothes that don't match. Yet when we get to know him better, we find that he is one of the nicest persons we've ever met. So we overlook how he chooses to dress, for that isn't half as important as how nice he is.

Or, let's say that a girl acts a bit strange—like eating peas with a knife or going for long walks in the rain—and we don't understand. Then we notice that she is always ready to help others. Now we view her differently. This strange behavior doesn't seem all that important anymore, for now we see how helpful she is.

Or, some girls and boys may think differently than we do. At first we may be shocked, and we wonder how they could think that way. Then we think again. Maybe they're right, and we're wrong. Anyhow, we do live in a free country, and they have as much right to their thoughts as we have to ours. So their different ideas have the right to be expressed, for in our kind of country we know how important that right is.

People are different. We think and act differently, and that's OK. Let's learn to be kind and accept each other, in spite of our differences.

In the Bible it says (from Proverbs): "Good sense makes [us] slow to anger, and it is [to our] glory to overlook an offense."

Let us pray.
Dear God: Help us to be more understanding of others. Amen.

No. 3

The Super Crush

I don't have to tell you what this can of pop I've brought in my brown bag stands for. You tell me. Right!

Aside from being just another can of pop called "Orange Crush®," this can reminds us of our favorite football team, the Denver Broncos. "Orange Crush" is also the name of their defensive team. You see, the Broncos wear orange shirts, and they crush the other team's offenses. You know that.

The Denver Broncos football team is very, very good—good enough to go all the way to the Super Bowl this year. For this reason I like to call them "the Super Crush." How many of you are going to watch our Denver Broncos win? They are going to win! You know that, and I know that, and soon the whole world will know that. Can there be any question that they are the best team? The question isn't whether or not they will win, but by how many points they will win. Isn't that the way you see it? Go Broncos! Go Broncos! Win! Win! Win!

But what if . . . they don't win? I know this is trying to think the impossible. No, it just can't happen. But what if something were to go wrong . . . like a referee making a mistake that helps the other team to win; or the ball bouncing the wrong way at the wrong time, allowing the other team to get just enough points to squeak by and win; or . . . Oh, I don't know what else could happen, but what if that something happens? How will we act then? Sad? Yes! Very sad! Disappointed? For sure! This will be the normal way to act. However, let me also suggest that we be our best selves if this should happen.

If Dallas wins, and you have a friend who is for the Cowboys, don't be angry or say things you would later regret. Be kind. Remember that this is how we would have wanted them to act if their team had lost. Also, as they say, "There's always next year." Like so many other disappointments in life, we have another chance next year. Think about that.

But, of course, the Broncos are going to win. Right? How will we feel? Happy! Very happy! You better believe it. But how will we act toward the boy and girl down the street or at school who is for Dallas? No, we must not rub it in, saying, "Our team beat your team, ha, ha, ha; our team beat your team, hee, hee, hee." Ah, once again we are going to be kind, yes, even polite.

After all, it's only a game. It's been said, "It's not whether you win or lose, but how you play the game."

Jesus said, "As you wish that [others] would do to you, do so to them." That means being a good loser as well as a good winner.

I have a friend who is for Dallas. When the Broncos win, I'm going to be nice about it, and if they were to . . . even then I'll be nice about it.

How about you?

Let us pray.
Dear God: Remind us to be good sports this day and every day. Amen.

Note: Dallas 27 and Denver 10

No. 4

Play It Again

Would you like to see something beautiful?
In my brown bag is a beautiful box,
colorfully painted. If we wanted to, we could spend
some time just looking at this box, admiring it from
every angle, from the top, the bottom, and the sides.
Whoever decorated it certainly did a beautiful job.

It belongs to Gayle. I gave it to her as an
anniversary present, which is a way of saying that I
am happy I'm married to her. She keeps it on her
dresser.

Do you know what kind of box this is? It's a
music box. To me it is a very special music box, not
only because of how beautifully it's painted, but also
because of the beautiful music it makes.

For it to play, the spring needs to be wound, like
this. Then you lift the top of the box, and the music
plays.

When I open the lid you can hear how beautiful that music is. Listen. This is the music from a movie called *Dr. Zhivago,* a movie that was made before many of you were born. This is the theme song, and it's one of my favorites. Also, it's one of Gayle's favorite songs. I could hear it again and again.

Something about this box causes me to listen to it often, and I never get tired of hearing it. I don't know who wrote the music, but whoever it was created a beautiful sound that must make God happy.

The same is true when we come to church. We hear again and again what we have heard before, and we sing time after time some of the same songs. Since we use some of the same ideas over and over, people might ask, "Don't you get tired of the same thing over and over again?"

Of course, we do like variety; we like some changes from time to time. Without change, it all could become dull and boring. We don't want that. However, while we want change to occur in order to keep our interest, there are some things we don't ever want to change.

For example, there is God's love for us. We don't grow tired of this, and we want to hear it again and again. You see, this is the most important thing we can hear or sing or say each Sunday when we come here. "God loves us."

Whenever you hear of God's love, don't merely think that you've heard it before; think also that you would like to hear it again and again. It's the most beautiful thing we can hear this side of heaven.

Let us pray.

Dear God: Let us hear again and again about your love for us. Amen.

No. 5

A Fuse

It happened yesterday. A big wedding was scheduled here at the church. With just twenty minutes to go, everyone was ready. I was checking over what I was going to say in the wedding when our church organist came to me and said, "The organ won't play."

What a jolt! It was almost time to start, and the organ wouldn't make a sound. Immediately I asked, "What do we do?" (I don't know very much about our big pipe organ.)

Calmly—I was glad someone was calm—she told me where to find the reset button for the organ. That's the button that starts the electricity going to the organ again, when for some reason it has been cut off. It's down in the cellar of the church. So, down I went, and I pushed it. Nothing happened. I pushed it again, this time holding it longer. Nothing. All the time I kept looking at my watch. It was fifteen minutes to go. Then it was ten minutes. Finally I came back up from the cellar.

One of the persons in the wedding said to me, "I bet you've blown a fuse!" She was right. Here's how it happened.

Over in that little office next to the sanctuary, where I do some of my studying during the week, there is a small electric heater. It had been on, and when the organ came on, it caused too much electricity to go through the fuse, thus causing the fuse to blow.

To make a long story short, we did finally find out which fuse it was (for a big building like this, there are so many!), but I'm sorry to say it was only after the wedding.

Judy, so that we can know the organ is OK again, would you please play a few notes. Thank you.

What's a fuse? I've bagged up the old fuse and brought it with me this morning—such a little thing for such a big bag.

A fuse is an electrical safety device which usually has a thin piece of metal in it that will melt if too much electricity goes through it. This fuse did what it was supposed to, because we were trying to send too much electricity through it when the heater and organ were going at the same time. It burned out and prevented any electricity from going through it. That's good, because if it hadn't, some serious harm could have happened to this big organ, perhaps a fire.

We have fuses in our own lives. No, we don't have this kind, made of glass, metal, and wire. Yet when troubles feed into our lives, more troubles than we can handle, we need some way to relieve the tension. Friends can be a fuse for us, helping to take the pressure off by sharing our troubles and giving us some good advice. Parents can be a fuse for us, helping us as our friends do, but even more so. The church can be a fuse for us, giving comfort and support and peace. But the most important fuse of all is prayer. It can give us help from God in dealing with troubles and difficulties. All this can keep us going, in spite of what may happen to us.

Ah, yes, from this fuse we can learn an important lesson: There is help for us when our troubles become too much for us.

Let us pray.

Dear God: Help us when our troubles are too much for us. Amen.

No. 6

Love, Love, Love

Thursday of this week is the big day when it comes to love. It's Valentine's Day. Are you ready? Have you chosen your valentines? February fourteenth is just a few days away.

That's why I've brought some pretty red paper and a pair of scissors in my brown bag. If you don't mind, I'm going to be a cut up—that is, with this paper.

Have you ever seen someone cut out paper dolls, the kind that hold hands? That's what I want to do with hearts.

First, I take this big sheet of red paper and begin folding it, back and forth, back and forth, like this. Notice, it looks like accordion folds.

Next, I take the scissors and cut out half a heart, making sure that on the big side of the heart I don't cut a complete semicircle. Instead I cut to the edge of the paper and then skip just a bit before starting to cut again.

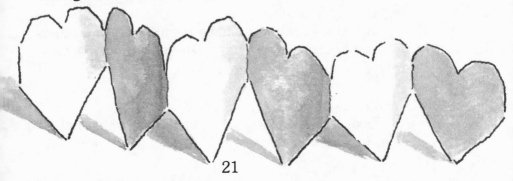

That sounds complicated, I know, but it isn't if you've watched me. There it is—a whole string of hearts.

Why am I doing this? It's not to show you how to cut out a string of hearts, although when you get home you may want to try this. Rather, I want to show that one heart is linked to another heart. Did you know that like these hearts our love is connected to the love of others? It's love, love, love, linked together.

Every year I send a valentine to my mother. Why? She loves me, and her love has caused me not only to love her in return but also to be more loving to others. Isn't that the way it is for you too?

The same is true with my family. They will receive valentines from me to tell them how much their love means to me.

Oh, there are many examples of how we have become more loving because we have been loved. Many schoolteachers and classmates, relatives and church members, strangers and friends, have in one way or another reached out to us with love. I love you, and I hope this makes a difference to you. Your love makes a difference to me.

The greatest love of all is spoken about in the Bible, "We love, because [God] first loved us." And it says, "Beloved, if God so loved us, we also ought to love one another."

Yes, God's love links us to others in a more loving way. Remember this when you give out your valentines this week.

We love because we have been loved, and others will love because they have been loved. Our hearts are linked together with love, love, love.

Let us pray.

Dear God: Thank you for loving us, which helps us to love others. Amen.

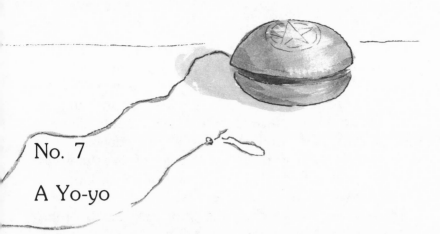

No. 7

A Yo-yo

How many of you have a yo-yo? I have one in my brown bag.

Since so many of you have yo-yos, I would venture to say that most, if not all of you, are better "yo-yoers" than I am.

It has been years since I took yo-yoing seriously. Oh, once in a while I'll pick up a yo-yo that belongs to one of our two children and try a few spins. Usually this is when no one is watching, for the way I yo-yo I don't want anyone watching.

But this morning is different—or I should say special—because I'm going to do a few spins while you watch me. My only request is that you be patient with me. Remember, I haven't practiced in a long time. Here goes.

Not bad, even if I say so myself. Of course, I can't do the tricks some people can, but maybe you're one of those who can perform the "Spinner," the "Walk the Dog," the "Over the Falls," or the "Around the World." I've seen these tricks done, so I know what I'm talking about, even though I can't do them.

In fact, I bet you could show me a trick or two if we had time. After church, let's meet outside and try a few tricks together with this yo-yo. I would like to learn from you, because I just do the basics—up and down, up and down. So it goes, and so it spins, except when the string gets all tangled up. Oh my, it looks as though it's beginning to do that now.

I've brought this yo-yo today to illustrate something special about God. Notice how the string keeps the yo-yo attached to the person controlling it. So it is with God and us. We're always attached to God, the One who controls more of our lives than we realize. In the Bible, God is spoken of as the One in whom "we live and move and have our being." That's true. The length of the string reminds us of the freedom we have to spin around in a lot of different ways. But we are always tied to God, for we have a basic dependence on God for such necessities as sunshine, water, food, and air. Without these, we couldn't live.

The yo-yo, when it's operating as it should, keeps coming back to where it started. And when we are doing as we should, we return to where we started. We are drawn back to God again and again, where we belong.

Of course, there are times when we get tangled up with ourselves. Then we spin out of control and finally just dangle there. We in the church use the word sin to explain this problem we have with ourselves. This is when we are apart from God. We need help if we are to get untangled and come back to God as we should.

All this from a yo-yo? Yes. So, when you wind up and let spin, think again about what you've heard this morning, of how the yo-yo tells us about God and ourselves.

Let us pray.
Dear God: Keep us close to you. Amen.

No. 8

Puppies and Parents

Where's my brown bag? You don't see it, do you? Yet, I do have a brown bag this morning. The reason I don't have it with me is that it's impossible for me to keep it behind the pulpit or beside my big chair as I sometimes do. It just wouldn't stay there. So, I've asked that my brown bag be brought to me. In a moment you'll see why. The bag, please.

Ah, sticking out of the bag is the head of a little puppy. May I introduce to you Brigadoon. We call him "Brig." He's the new arrival in our house, nine weeks old. Brig is a Bearded Collie.

Isn't he cute? When grown, he will have a silver color, with hair coming down in front of his eyes. That doesn't mean he won't be able to see; he'll be able to see, in spite of the hair.

Speaking of hair, since this was to be his first trip to church—and no doubt his last—our family gave him a bath last night so he would be clean for this "show and tell." As far as we know, it was his first bath ever, and he acted so nice about it. He smells so good!

This is our first dog, and we're learning how to care for him—when to feed him, when to take him outside, and when to say "no" to him. Now, Brig is a smart dog. He's beginning to learn what we want him to do. Oh, he still forgets from time to time, but he's learning. We must train him to be a good dog.

I've been thinking a lot about training the past week. Brig made me think about when I was young. My parents took the time to care for me, to see to it that I was raised correctly. Of course, there is a lot more to raising a child than raising a dog (no offense, Brig). My parents did so much for me! And I thank them. I know Brig is unable to thank us, except with a wag of his tail and with those wet kisses he gives us.

Are you thankful for what your parents do for you? They have an important job helping you grow up as you should. Yes, you need to be thankful for all they are doing for you.

When you get home, remember what we've talked about, and tell your parents how much you thank them for all they have done for you.

Then, in your prayers, thank God for your parents.

Let us pray.

Dear God: We are thankful for puppies and parents. Amen.

No. 9

Spelled with an *i* and an *e*

This morning there is a special brush in my brown bag. What makes this brush so special? Sure, you've seen your mom or dad use one like this. It's used to get lint off clothes. Here, let me show you how it's used on my pants (that is, if I can find them underneath this robe—ah, there they are). It's easy, just brush, brush, brush.

Wait a minute. What is "lint," *l-i-n-t*? Right. It's a soft, fleecy fuzz that comes from linen or cotton. It clings, and you have to brush it off. If you don't have a brush, there are other ways of removing lint. I could use tape. Since tape is sticky, it takes off lint easily. Or you can buy lint removers that are made with special material to roll lint away. Anyway, when you have lint, you want to get it off one way or another. I prefer the brush.

What is "Lent," *L-e-n-t*? Now this is a word different from the one we've been talking about so far. I have written both words out for you. Take a look.

What does this word Lent mean? Lent is the forty days before Easter, not counting Sundays. We are now in the lenten season of our church year. During this time we begin our preparation for Easter by remembering what happened to Jesus, how he suffered and died and then came to life again. It is also a time when we take a careful look at ourselves to see if we have been good or bad or just so-so. We ask God to forgive us for what we have done wrong, and we then try to live the way God wants us to live.

The word Lent comes from a very old English word, *lencten,* which means "springtime." It is used as a way of saying we need to come alive again.

We know what happens in the springtime. The flowers and trees and grass seem to come alive. During the winter months, nothing seems to grow. That is why this word Lent was used to describe this time of year.

Winter will soon be over, and then nature will burst out with new life. What will soon be happening in nature is what should be happening in us. No, we don't turn green and grow flowers out of our ears. Rather, we need to become alive again to the best way to live. When that happens, then we become new persons.

God makes the plants become new, of course. And it is God who helps us to become new again, by forgiving us for the wrong things we've done and by loving us until we see and do what is right.

During Lent we talk about how God wants us to start over again to become new people. So, when we hear this word Lent, *L-e-n-t,* let's think not of the fuzz on clothes but of how God wants to make us new again.

Let us pray.
Dear God: We want to be new again. Amen.

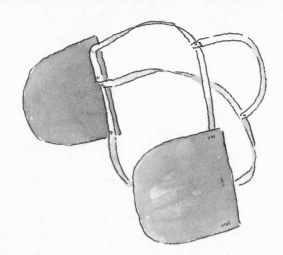

No. 10

Horse Blinders

Temptation. What does that word mean? It means wanting to do something that is wrong.

It reminds me of the fourth grade, in Mrs. Ratzlaff's room. She was a good teacher, and I'll never forget her.

We would be working at our desks on spelling or math. She would remind us to do our own work. But then there would be some wandering eyes. Do you know what that means? Some would look around for the correct answer, saying to themselves, "How do you spell . . . ? Well, let's see how Tommy has spelled it," or "What's the answer to this math problem? Maybe Sue has it already figured out." So, they yield to the temptation to look.

I hope you don't do that! Did I? Well . . . Unfortunately, I must have, or else this wouldn't stand out in my mind as it does. Now I'm sorry I did!

Very little got by Mrs. Ratzlaff. She always seemed to notice when someone tried to sneak a peek at someone else's paper. When the temptation was too much for us, she would say—without calling any names and usually from her desk without looking up—"I'm going to put some horse blinders on some of you!"

Horse blinders? What did she mean? Any idea?

Let me show you. I don't have real horse blinders with me this morning (I haven't seen a pair of

29

those in years, except at the state fair). But last night I made a pair. They're in my brown bag.

Do you want to see what they look like on? I'll put them on if you'll promise not to laugh. There. Ah, you laughed! That's OK for they are funny-looking, aren't they? Real horse blinders are made of leather and are bigger than these I've made out of cardboard and strips of cloth. The purpose of blinders is to keep horses from seeing something out of the corner of their eyes that would frighten them. Mrs. Ratzlaff meant to tell us that the blinders would keep us from looking out of the corners of our eyes at our neighbor's paper. Get the idea?

Of course, we all are tempted in many ways—every day. We may be tempted to cheat. Or we may be tempted to take something that doesn't belong to us. Or we may be tempted not to tell the whole truth, for fear we'll get ourselves into more trouble. Or we may be tempted to do something that would be mean and unfair to someone. There are many, many ways we are tempted to do what is wrong. Say "No!" to those tempting thoughts.

Jesus told his followers that they must not give in to temptation, that they must not say "Yes" when temptation comes. He said: "Watch and pray that you may not enter into temptation; the spirit indeed is willing, but the flesh is weak." This means that while we may not want to say "Yes" to temptation, yet we often do say "Yes." So, we need to watch out that this doesn't happen, praying to God for the help we need to stand strong.

Let us pray.
Dear God: Help us to be strong when we are tempted to do what is wrong. Amen.

No. 11

Smoothing Out the Rough Places

What is it? It looks like paper, but it's really more than paper. When I turn it over, you can tell what it is—sandpaper. In my brown bag I have some cut in small squares for each of you. Take one.

Rub the sandpaper between your fingers. Rough? Sure it is. That's why we call it sandpaper and why it's so valuable. By taking sand and gluing it onto a piece of paper in a way that the sand is kept from easily coming off, it makes an important tool for anyone who works with wood. With it we can make a rough surface become smooth.

I'm rather partial to sandpaper. You see, I work with wood and I need a lot of sandpaper to do the job right.

There's a lesson from this sandpaper I want you to learn. At times, your life may be rough around the edges and you may need some smoothing out if you are to be better.

Maybe it's the way you hold your fork when you eat peas, and mom and dad have to say to you, "Hold your fork this way." At that moment a touch of "human sandpaper" has helped to smooth you out, and you begin to have better table manners.

Maybe you aren't doing your schoolwork as you should—not getting done what the teacher has assigned or doing sloppy handwriting on a paper—and the teacher has to correct you. When you make the necessary corrections, then you are being smoothed out a bit more, so that you will become a better student.

Maybe your room is messy, and you have to be told to clean it up. If you do as you are told and keep on doing as you're told, a rough part of your life has been smoothed.

Maybe you aren't as nice as you should be to the boy or girl across the street, and you need to learn what it means to be a friend again. When that lesson is learned, then some smoothing out of your rough places has happened.

How do I know about your rough places? Well, I too was young once. Those who cared enough—my parents, friends, and teachers—began helping me to smooth out the rough places in my life, and this is still happening to me, as it is to you. We all need that smoothing touch.

A phrase in the Bible comes to mind when I think about rough things. It says, ". . . And the rough places shall be made smooth." That passage is about Jesus coming to help persons like you and me to live better.

When Jesus comes into our lives, then the rough places can be made smooth. This means more than just better table manners or cleaning up a messy room—important as these concerns are as we grow up. Rather, this smoothing begins when we are more loving, more caring, more giving of ourselves to help others. Yes, there have been times when we haven't been as loving, as caring, as giving as we should have been, and we need some smoothing out. That's what Jesus came to do, and will do for us if we let him.

So, feel this sandpaper and think about all the ways you need to be smoothed out.

Let us pray.
Dear God: Through Jesus, make smooth the rough places in our lives. Amen.

No. 12

Removing That Stain

Some time ago I took a suit to the cleaners. On it was a not-so-nice-looking stain. When I picked up the suit a few days later, the stain was still there. "Why?" I asked. The lady told me it was a stain they couldn't get out. I didn't argue with her about it, although I did tell her I thought the stain could be removed—somehow.

I was determined to prove the stain could be removed. So when I arrived home I used a stain and spot remover. It worked! I have it in my brown bag this morning. K2r. How many of you have K2r at home?

I want to warn you not to use it yourselves. Let your parents use it for you. It says right on the tube, KEEP OUT OF REACH OF CHILDREN. Why? Because if you were to get it on your hands and put your hands up to your eyes or in your mouth, that could be dangerous. So, let mom or dad use it for you.

Here, let me show you how it works. I've put some butter on this piece of cloth. Let's pretend I've

dropped it from a piece of toast. I want to get the stain out. With this K2r I go to work, rubbing it in and then waiting for it to dry. While it's drying, let me first clean my fingers, for I certainly don't want to get it in my eyes or mouth accidentally. When this dries and turns white and powdery, I'll brush it off, and the stain will be gone.

Yesterday, while thinking about God's forgiveness, I thought about K2r. Of course, they don't work the same way at all, except that both can remove the stains in our lives. K2r lifts the stains out of our clothes, while God's forgiveness lifts the stain of sin out of our lives. You see, when we don't do what God wants us to do, we sin. This may mean not being as loving and kind toward others as we should be, or being too self-centered, or not believing and trusting in God as fully as we ought. This makes a stain on our lives, a not-so-happy feeling that we have done something wrong. If we ask, God will forgive us.

Forgiveness means we are loved so much that God wants to forget about what we have done wrong. But first we must ask God to forgive us. Then it happens. The stain of sin in our lives is lifted up and out.

K2r works to remove stains in our clothes. Let's brush away this white powdery stuff that is left after it dries. Look, the stain is gone!

God's forgiveness works to remove sin from our lives. The stains of wrongdoing and sin are gone!

Let us pray.
Dear God: For all the wrongs that have stained our lives, we are sorry; and we pray that these stains may be removed through your forgiveness. Amen.

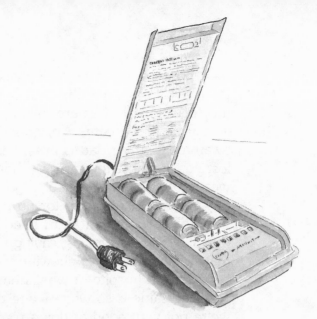

No. 13

All Charged Up

"I need to have my batteries charged." And there are two ways to do this.

In my brown bag is a battery charger. No, it's not like the big charger they have down at the service station which charges car batteries. This charger is smaller. Here's what it looks like. And here's how it works.

Let's take these old batteries from my flashlight. There's no power in them. They're dead! I used to buy new batteries when this happened, but not now. Instead of throwing these old batteries away, I put them in here. Before I do that, take a look inside.

We see wires, springs, and two compartments. At one end is a light that goes on when the batteries are ready to be used again, and on the other end is an electrical cord. The instructions are found in the top of the lid.

Let's see, for these batteries, size C, I'll need to leave them in this charger for nine to fourteen hours, or for a quick charge about two hours. When the batteries have been charged with new power and are ready to be used again, this yellow light comes on.

But there's another way I need to have my batteries charged. I'm talking about the inside of me—not what goes inside my flashlight. For example, there are times when I'm sad. Surely you know how this feels, for all of us are unhappy at times. For you, it may be that a very, very good friend has moved away, or mom or dad is upset with you, or you've lost your favorite toy, or it's a holiday and the weather is too bad for you to go out to play, or—you're just unhappy for no reason at all.

That's when you and I need to be charged up! A friend can do this for us, saying just the right thing to make us feel better or showing us how we can be happy again in spite of what's happened.

The same is so when we're discouraged because we're not very good at doing something. Maybe we've failed many times, or maybe we've overheard someone question whether or not we're able to do what we'd like to do, such as playing on the team.

Yes, it's so easy to think "I'm no good!" and then be discouraged with ourselves. At these times we need to be recharged, so that we'll be more positive about ourselves. We may be able to recharge ourselves by giving ourselves a pep talk or listening to a friend who believes in us and charges us up.

The same is true with our faith in God. There are times when it's hard to believe, because God seems far away and our prayers don't get answered as soon as we think they should. That's when we need to come to church and get charged up so that we can believe again.

I think of those words from the Bible, "Let your light so shine . . ." You and I can do this when our batteries of happiness, self-confidence, and faith are charged up. For the light to shine, let's get our personal batteries charged and recharged.

Let us pray.
Dear God: Keep our batteries charged, that our light might shine. Amen.

The year of our Lord **April** nineteen hundred seventy-nine

SUNDAY	MONDAY	TUESDAY	WEDNESDAY	THURSDAY	FRIDAY	SATURDAY
1	2	3	4	5	6	7
8	9	10	11	12	13	14
15	16	17	18	19	20	21
22	23	24	25	26	27	28
29	30					

No. 14

Foolin'?

Did you know that there won't be any more school for the rest of the year?

There are free toys for everyone at the end of the worship service today.

What's that bug doing in your hair?

Look, you have different-colored socks on—one black and one brown.

Next Sunday we're going to have a circus at church, and a man is going to swing from those beams up there.

Did any of you see my pet snake? It's crawling somewhere around here on the floor.

I've brought a calendar in my brown bag this morning, and this calendar has today circled in red. Why? Sure, it's April Fools' Day. Those funny little grins on your faces tell me you know all about this day. Give me a few examples of how you have been foolin' your family and friends.

Fun, isn't it? It's most fun when you really fool someone and then say, "April fool!" You see, the person believing you is called an "April fool."

Why do we say this? It began over four hundred years ago in a country called France. At that time the first day of the year was April first, but the king of France decided to change the start of the new year to January first. Those who forgot about the change and who still thought of April first as New Year's Day were

37

called "April fools." That started the idea of fooling people on the first day of April. Ever since, people have made this a day for fooling others. That's OK, provided we are doing it just for fun.

But there is also a time for us to be truthful. Even on an April Fools' Day like this it isn't OK to lie for the sake of lying—or as a way of getting ourselves out of trouble. It's important to tell the truth. If we don't, we lie, and we know that's wrong.

When we read the Bible, it becomes very clear that it is important for us to be truthful in all we say and do. Here are some of the words from the Bible about truth that I read just yesterday:

"Do not lie to one another."

"Love the truth."

"Speak the truth to one another."

"Know the truth."

"Live according to the truth."

"Know that no lie is of the truth."

"Children, let us not love in word or speech but in deed and in truth."

God wants us to be truthful.

Of course, today is special. We can play our April Fools' jokes, and that's OK. But let's not forget when to tell the truth.

Let us pray.

Dear God: In all we say and do, may we become more truthful. Amen.

No. 15

Thumbs Up

Let's play "Simon Says." Ready? Do everything that Simon tells you to do and nothing more.

Simon says, "Thumbs up."
Simon says, "Thumbs down."
Simon says, "Thumbs up."
"Thumbs down."

Caught you, didn't I? Simon didn't say "Thumbs down." I did. Want to try it again? Here we go. Remember, do just what Simon tells you to do.

Have you ever thought about thumb language? You know, you do and say a lot with a thumb. For example, you can hitchhike a ride with a thumb, you can thumb your nose at someone (which isn't a very nice thing to do), you can use it with the forefinger to make tweezers, you can call a runner out at home plate if you are the umpire, you can put it in your mouth and suck it, you can put it in a pie and pull out a plum (you know how that story goes). But there is another use of the thumb I want to talk about this morning.

What does it mean to put your thumb down? Like this. It's a way of saying you disapprove of something. It's also a way of saying "Die!" without using that word. Back in the days of the early Christians, the Romans often threw people they didn't like into a big arena (some of these people were

39

Christians), and the crowd would use their thumbs to show what they wanted done. If the crowd put their thumbs down, it meant death (either by sword or by lions). If they put their thumbs up, it meant the prisoners could live. Remember, this happened thousands of years ago, but we still know what "thumbs down" means. And we still turn thumbs down when we don't approve of something, even though it doesn't mean death now.

Of course, thumbs up means approval, like "It's OK!" or "Let them live!" We still do this today.

Today, Easter Day, is a "thumbs up" day all the way. The reason is that when Jesus died, God made it possible for him to live again. God turned thumbs up when others were turning thumbs down. And God won out, making this a "thumbs up" day.

This is why we celebrate Easter. Jesus was alive again after he died on the cross, and God made it happen. Remember that, will you?

To help you remember, I have something in my brown bag for each of you. It's a big hand with the thumb turned up. And you and I know why. On the back of the hand is written, "He is risen!"

Let us pray.

Dear God: Thank you for making this a "thumbs up" day for Jesus, and promising to do the same for us when we die. Amen.

No. 16

It Was a Hat

We were getting ready for that big day—Easter. Since it is such a special day, we wanted to look our best. A new dress was being made for Suzanne. It was a long, old-fashioned-looking dress. Her mother worked hard on it, and when it was finished, it looked beautiful. Yet something more was needed. A hat—that was what she needed with this new dress. Her last year's straw hat looked just right with it. So, on Easter morning she wore the dress, but not the hat. Why?

On Friday before Easter, our family was not at home for part of the day. When we came home, we had a big surprise. We walked in, and there in the living room was our favorite dog—our only dog—and he was having a good time with that hat. He had torn it to pieces! Suzanne had left the hat on the bedpost, and Brig had left it on the living room floor.

Let me show you what is left, for I have the pieces in my brown bag. I'll even try it on for you—which isn't easy. It was a hat, but now it's more like a pile of straw.

In all fairness to Brig (his full name is Brigadoon, and I think at that moment we used his full name, plus a few other names), it needs to be said that he is just a puppy. He's still in his chewing stage of life, not having grown old enough to know better. When he is older, we plan to train him to be a nice, obedient dog. Oh, we still love him, in spite of what he has done. He didn't know he was doing anything wrong when he went to work on this hat.

What he did caused me to start thinking about something else. There certainly are a lot of things destroyed in our city and world that shouldn't be. I once knew a boy who loved shooting out streetlights with his BB gun. That wasn't me! Maybe you know people who like to destroy things that don't belong to them. It happens all the time, and we call it "vandalism." Have you ever heard that word before? Sure you have. It means destroying something that doesn't belong to you. Unfortunately, there are too many people who do this. Some may be too young to know better, but most who vandalize are old enough to know better. Still, they do it—as they say, "for the fun of it." It's so sad and so maddening.

I know you wouldn't do that. You know better! You've been taught by your parents to respect what belongs to someone else, and that's good. This is what we also teach here at church, for it's a very important way of showing love for others.

I hope Brig has learned his lesson. If he needs more instructions on how a good dog should act, I'll teach him. As for you, you know the right thing to do when it comes to respecting what belongs to others, and that's good.

Let us pray.
Dear God: May we always respect what belongs to others. Amen.

Dear Rev. Jordan
During our church school class last
Sunday we discussed "Helpers in the
Church." In our story Phoebe helped
Paul by taking a letter to the
Christians in Rome. As a class project
we thought you might like to have
a letter from us. We like to listen
to you every Sunday and love you
very much. May God Bless you   Love

Lisa   Love   Suzanne
       Julie Michelle Geoff
       Gretchen Patrice   STACI
       Brian   Erin
       Katie
       emily   JUSTIN

Pre School Class 4-5

No. 17

A Church Letter

Last Monday I received a wonderful letter. It was from some of you, from those of you in the four- and five-year-old class. I have it in my brown bag, and I would like to read it.

> Dear Rev. Jordan,
>   During our church school class last Sunday we discussed "Helpers in the Church." In our story Phoebe helped Paul by taking a letter to the Christians in Rome. As a class project we thought you might like to have a letter from us. We like to listen to you every Sunday and love you very much. May God Bless You.
>   Love,

And this letter is signed: Lisa, Suzanne, Julie, Michelle, Geoff, Stacy, Gretchen, Patrick, Brian, Erin, Katie, Emily, Justin.
    Thank you for this letter. It makes me very happy. In fact, it's one of those letters I plan to save.
    Those of you who signed my letter mentioned that you were studying about helpers in the church. It pleases me that you have talked about this.
    We have many helpers in this church. Your church school teachers are helping you to learn more and more about God, about Jesus, and about how

43

you are to live as you should—with love. There are those in our church who take care of the church's building, keeping it in repair, so when it rains we don't have raindrops falling on our heads. There are those who do many other necessary jobs in the church, from handling the money you give (so it will be spent wisely—as God would want it spent) to singing in the choir, from planning special events like vacation church school and church dinners to cutting the church lawn, from helping needy strangers who come to the church to ushering on Sunday mornings.

I think of myself as a helper in the church, and I also think of you in this way. There are many things you can do to help: be kind and loving, sing in the youth choir, take up the offering in your church school class, draw the bulletin covers during Advent and Lent (those are the times before Christmas and Easter), being an acolyte (some of you will have to be a little older before you can do this). In your church school class you may want to talk further about how you can work in the church.

A helper in the church is a marvelous thing to be. And you are helpers. We all are. By doing this, we are workers for God. Always remember this.

You ended your letter to me with, "We . . . love you very much. May God Bless You." That is exactly what I want to say to you. "I love you very much. May God Bless You."

Let us pray.
Dear God: May we be good helpers in the church. Amen.

No. 18

Let There Be Light and Colors

How many of you like to paint? It's fun! When I was your age, I had my own set of watercolors, and I really painted up a storm. That means I did a lot of painting.

I haven't watercolored in a long time. A member of our church, Mary Lou Anderson, offered to teach a class in watercoloring. So, last Wednesday the class had its first lesson. Maybe I'll become good enough to do a painting worth hanging at home—in the bathroom, in my study, or maybe in the living room.

Before we put our brushes to paper, we talked about colors. Did you know there are only three basic colors? They are red, yellow, and blue. From these three, we get our other colors—by mixing them. For example, if you mix yellow and red, you get orange; or blue and yellow, you get green; or red and blue, you get violet. And when you can take some of these new colors, mix them with other colors you've mixed, you'll get other shades of colors. Then you can paint all the different colors you see in God's world, from sunrises to sunsets, from trees to flowers, from mountains to valleys.

But do we make these colors? We don't really, even though we may mix them together. God makes the colors. How do we know this? Of course, God made the world, and since colors are part of the world, then God must have made colors. It just stands to reason.

In my brown bag I have a prism. How many of you have ever seen a prism? It's a special piece of glass, cut so that the light comes in, bends, and then comes out, showing that in light there are all the colors of the rainbow. Let's see if we can see these colors through this prism. Over there is a sunbeam coming through the window. Follow me.

Now, everyone stand right here and watch as I hold this prism just right, reflecting the colors in the light off of this big piece of white poster board. There we are. Tell me, what colors do you see? Good! Those are all the colors of the rainbow. Now let's go sit down again and talk about what we've seen and why we saw it.

When the sunbeam shone through the prism, the light was bent in such a way that we could see colors. Did you know there are colors in light? There are! That's what is happening when we see a rainbow in the sky. This doesn't mean that there is a great big prism up there doing this to the light. Little drops of water act like a prism, bending the light and thus showing the colors in it.

Remember, our colors come from God, and what a wondrous God we have.

In the Bible it says, "And God said, 'Let there be light.'" That was the beginning of color in God's world. Think about what this world would be like without colors—no reds, yellows, blues, or any of the other mixtures of these basic three. God wanted a colorful world, and we should give God our thanks—often—for colors.

Let us pray.
Dear God: For red, yellow, blue, and all the other colors, we thank you. Amen.

46

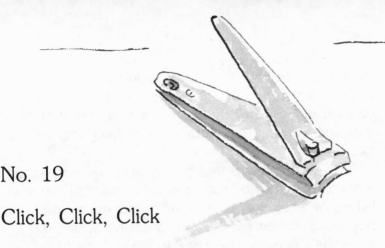

No. 19

Click, Click, Click

I like to look nice when I come to church, and I know you do too. So, before coming, I take a shower, shave my beard, comb my hair, brush my teeth, make sure my pants are pressed (although it doesn't make much difference with this robe on, does it?), polish my shoes, check my fingernails, and so on.

Speaking of fingernails, I clipped mine this morning, for they had grown long (I've been drinking my milk). Hey, that's not quite right, for I only clipped one hand. See, here's the other hand. Looking at the two, you can see one has been clipped and the other hasn't. In my brown bag, I have my pair of fingernail clippers. If you don't mind, I'll clip them right now.

Wait a minute! This is no place to do that. I've been taught that it's not good manners to clip your fingernails in the company of others. That's something you should do at home when you're alone. So I had better wait until later to do this, even though it's uncomfortable to have the fingernails on one hand longer than those on the other hand.

There is another reason why it's better not to clip fingernails in public, whether it's at church, at school, in a crowd, or wherever there are other people. Leaving manners to the side (for just a minute), the clicking of the clippers can be very annoying. I don't like to hear it. It really gets on my nerves. I've seen people do this when someone was speaking, and those trying to hear what the speaker was saying began instead to hear only that click, click, click. It got on their nerves, too, causing them to be upset and annoyed, wishing that whoever was doing that would stop.

Do we do things that get on people's nerves? Oh, it doesn't have to be with a pair of fingernail clippers. When we chew ice, or tap our fingers on the desk, or pop gum, or you name it, we could be getting on someone's nerves. There are so many ways to unnerve others. Sure, some things are all right to do in the right place at the right time, but when we know they bother others, it's wrong to do them or to keep doing them after we find out how it makes others feel. Not to take into account feelings of others would be unloving and rude.

Paul was right when he said, "Love is not rude." That's in the Bible.

So, I'll wait until I get home to clip my nails, and now you know why.

Let us pray.

Dear God: Help us to be more aware of the feelings of others. Amen.

No. 20

A Hairy Subject

I saw this in the newspaper the other day:

> How many individual hairs do you (or did you)
> have on your head? It varies according to hair
> color. Redheads—80,000. Brunettes—100,-
> 000. Blondes—120,000.

Now I know. I've 80,000 hairs on my head. But
maybe I have less hair, for I'm getting older, and it's
beginning to look a bit thinner here in front. That's
OK, though, for less hair means fewer problems,
especially with the price of haircuts these days.

How many of you have red or reddish hair?
You're an 80,000 person. You brunettes, I've got
your number, and the same for you blondes.
However, I wonder about you who have black hair.
The newspaper article didn't tell about you. Do you
have more or less than I have?

Since I've been told I'm thinning out up here,
maybe I should do something about it. In my brown
bag I have a "hairy" solution. Close your eyes for just
a few seconds and I'll show you. OK, open wide.
How do you like my wig? I wonder how many hairs
are in this wig. Let's count them. No, we don't have
time to do that. Does it really matter how many hairs
are in this wig? Not to me!

This wig, however, does remind me of a very

important fact: The exact number of hairs I have on my head is known, and it is the same for you. It doesn't matter what color our hair is or how much or how little we have to comb. Every last hair is numbered.

It says in the Bible, "Why, even the hairs of your head are all numbered." And who has done the counting? God, of course! God knows how many hairs are on our heads, and that's good to know. You see, this says a lot about God and us.

God knows everything. Naturally, it's God's business to know everything, from how many trees there are to how many grains of sand there are, from how many stars there are in the heavens to how many frogs there are in a pond, from how many humans there are to how many hairs we all have on our heads. After all, God made everything, so—.

This also says to us that God knows each one of us. For example, if God knows the number of hairs on our heads, then God knows us personally—which means that God knows everything about us, name and address, likes and dislikes, troubles and joys. Yes, God does more than just count our hairs.

This also tells us that we're of great value to God. If we weren't valuable to God, would God have gone to all the trouble of counting the hairs on our heads? Think about that!

And, finally, this reminds us that we are loved by God. That's what Jesus was trying to tell us when he told us about hairs on our heads.

The next time you comb your hair, remember this. Then say a prayer of thanks to God, who knows and loves us so well. Why should we wait? Let's tell God now.

Let us pray.
Dear God: Thank you for loving us so much that the hairs of our heads are numbered. Amen.

50

No. 21

The Language of Love

Last weekend was special for our church. As you know, we had visitors from afar—Japan. There were thirty-seven high school students and two sponsors.

It was fun. How many of you had some of these Japanese young people in your home?

We had two in our home; their first names were Shu and Fumisato. Shu could speak better English than Fumisato, but Fumisato could understand English better than Shu. Working together they could understand us fairly well, and this allowed us to talk about many things, like "What is life like in Japan?" and "What do you think of the way we live here?" We talked and laughed a lot. Even though the time was short, we felt we were able to get to know them very well, and they were able to know us too. When they left last Monday morning, we wanted to cry. In fact, I think I saw some teary eyes. Mine were.

This experience was great for us. Now when we think of the Japanese people, we'll naturally think of the students who came to visit us. We now have a friendship with them, but even more, we have a love for them.

You know, their coming to our church was good for us all. I had several church members say they felt this helped to bring us closer together, causing us to be friendlier with one another, more loving. I think so too.

Last Sunday evening many people came to the church for the dinner we gave for our visitors. Before the dinner, our visitors demonstrated some of the ways they do things: arranging flowers (beautiful!); folding paper to make birds, animals, flowers, boxes, hats, boats (fascinating!); explaining how they do their math (different!); showing how they brew and drink tea (interesting!); and writing their language (wow!).

Some of us had our names written in Japanese. I did, and I've brought it in my brown bag to show you. I know it says this because they said so. I also asked for something else to be written in Japanese, the word friendship. Here is what it looks like. Here's another one. Would you like to guess what it says? It's the word for "love." Their sponsor told me this means the kind of love God has for us as well as the kind of love we have as friends.

Last weekend we learned better how to love one another, even though we may be different in many ways.

That's what Jesus taught. He said, "This I command you, to love one another."

Let us pray.

Dear God: Thank you for this opportunity to love others. Amen.

No. 22

What to Do About Greener Grass

It's been said, "The grass is always greener on the other side of the fence." Tell me what that means.

In my brown bag I have a plastic bag. By looking through the plastic you can tell what's in it—grass. Here, let me slip out this clump for you to see even better.

Can you guess where it came from? Not my yard, no way! It's from my neighbor's yard. Oh, he said it was OK. There isn't a fence between our front yards, just a long, low hedge. When I look over, I see greener grass in his yard, and I want his grass instead of mine.

Do you see the problem? Yes, I want what my neighbor has. Of course, there is nothing wrong with that, except when my wants get out of control. Let me explain, for this idea applies to more than just grass.

Maybe you have been over to a friend's house recently, and that friend has many, many new toys and games. You enjoy playing there, but you come home thinking that your toys aren't much fun. What your friend has is what you want, and you want it now!

Let's say you have another friend who can think a lot faster and better than you can, and this causes you to feel a bit slow. Or, your friend may be better at some sport or may play a musical instrument better

53

than you. So you become very, very sad because you can't perform like your friend can.

Perhaps your friend has more opportunities to do things and to go places, and you feel cheated. You become angry with your parents and jealous of your friend.

In the Bible there is a word for this strong wanting what someone else has. It's "covet." It means having a strong desire for what belongs to another. And we learn from reading the Bible that we must guard against coveting. But how?

Well, first of all, if it's a toy or something you can carry, you don't take it. You simply say to yourself, "It doesn't belong to me, and I can't have it." No one can have everything, and you shouldn't fret yourself sick over wanting what someone else has.

After you have talked to yourself, you can think about what you have, and you will probably realize that you already have more than you first thought.

And if you still covet what someone else has, you can always talk with me or your parents. We will understand, and perhaps we can help you feel differently.

Of course, you can turn to God and ask for help when you begin to covet what belongs to someone else. God will help you!

Yes, the grass often seems greener on the other side of the fence. But don't let coveting get the best of you or take the best out of you.

Let us pray.
Dear God: Keep us from coveting what others have. Amen.

No. 23

That Fly!

The other day I was at my desk studying when suddenly a big fly buzzed me. It wasn't just a normal housefly. No, this was a big fellow. He (I think it was a he, or maybe it was a she; oh, I don't know which, for I don't know how to tell—do you?), he or she, as the case may be, could fly fast and make the loudest-sounding buzz. Maybe it would help if I showed you this fly. Let's get the jar from my brown bag. Here we are.

It wasn't easy to catch this fly. The normal housefly can travel four and a half miles per hour, and even faster when it's excited.

My first reaction was not to catch this fly at all. I can remember saying to it, "Oh, buzz off!" Because it was really bothering me! I found myself just sitting, not doing my work, and watching this fly flit here and there. It flew so fast that it bumped into things, like the wall, the door, the window.

My second reaction was to get up and give it a great big swat and thus get rid of it once and for all.

But then I thought more kindly toward this big, old fly. Now, I don't particularly like flies, but I was more kind to this one than I normally am to flies. The thought crossed my mind that flies do have a purpose or God wouldn't have made them. What do you think this purpose might be?

One important thing flies do is help things that

have died to rot and decay faster, thus returning them to the earth to be used again in new plants and life. Or the little fruit fly—which this one isn't—has been a help to us in the study of heredity, a big word which helps us to understand why we get blue eyes instead of brown eyes, why we look like dad or mom, why we may be tall or short. You see, the study of the fruit fly can help us better understand ourselves. Also, flies become food for some of God's other creatures, like birds, spiders, and frogs. If we were to check out all the ten thousand different kinds of flies there are, we could find a lot more answers to why God made flies.

I also warn you that flies are some of the most dangerous insects known to us. They carry germs, and germs make people sick. Remember that when you see a fly. That's why we swat flies.

But I didn't swat this one, because it caused me to think of an important truth. Where there is bad, we should also look for the good. That doesn't mean we are saying that bad is good. No way! Rather, there are some good things we can say about this fly and there are some bad things too.

So it is with people. Most people are good, and we have no problem with them, but others remind us of this fly, pesty and not good. We would like to tell them to "buzz off" or swat them right between the eyes. But we should always look for their good points and love them. That's what God does. That's a lesson to learn, to look for the good we can love.

Hey, thank you for "flying" with me this morning.

Let us pray.
Dear God: Help us to see the good in others. Amen.

No. 24

Fool's Gold

Recently our family went up into the mountains for a short vacation. We had fun together, doing and seeing many things. Let me tell you about one of the things we did.

We were in an old mining town called Silverton, Colorado. Miners have been working around that area for about a hundred years, digging for gold, silver, and some other minerals. It's all very interesting.

From where we were staying, we could see an old gold mine that hadn't been worked for over thirty years. It was way up on the side of a mountain. As a family we decided to hike up to it, and we did—with much huffing and puffing.

While we were up there we found the rock I have in my brown bag. Here, take a look at it. See how it sparkles. It looks like gold. After all, it was found up near that old gold mine. Do you think it's gold?

It's not. It's called "iron pyrite," or "fool's gold." Real gold is worth a lot. This is worth nothing.

There are many stories about people finding rocks like this one. They think they have struck it rich, and they have to be told, "Sorry, it's only fool's gold." They thought they had the real thing, but actually they had only been fooled.

So goes a lot of life. Often we think we have found something of great value, only to find out later we were wrong.

Sometimes it's a toy. By getting it, we think we'll be the happiest person ever. But soon it's broken, not because we were overly rough with it but because it wasn't well made. We were fooled.

Sometimes we have an idea that we want to try, like eating all the ice cream and candy we desire, and when we do we find it isn't as great as we thought, especially when we get sick. We were fooled.

Sometimes it's being told we've a true friend, only to find out later that that person has said mean and unkind things about us to others. We were fooled.

Sometimes we think life would be great if only mom or dad did everything for us, and then we find out it's not the best way to grow up. We were fooled.

Oh, it's easy to be fooled some of the time, but God doesn't want us to be fooled. God wants us to learn the truth while we live, so we can know what is of value and what isn't. It's all part of growing up as we should. Let's not be fooled!

Remember, not all that glitters is gold, nor is everything that attracts us good for us.

Let us pray.
Dear God: Help us not to be fooled. Amen.

No. 25

Getting a Good Grip

How many of you looked at Pikes Peak this morning? That mountain does things to me! It's beautiful and so inviting. I like to look at it and remember a climb I made recently.

Oh, yes. I've climbed Pikes Peak several times. A couple of weeks ago I climbed it again. It's not easy! Even though it's not the highest mountain in Colorado, it's said to be one of the hardest to climb. The reason is that you have to start climbing at a lower altitude than when you climb most of the other tall mountains in our state. You start at about seven thousand feet above sea level and climb to a little over fourteen thousand feet. Also, it's thirteen miles to the top. Sure, there's a path all the way up, but it's not easy. Halfway up I always say to myself, "Why am I doing this?" My feet hurt, my ankles hurt, my legs hurt, my hips hurt, my back hurts, my lungs hurt—I just hurt all over.

Why do I climb Pikes Peak? Because it's there! Also, because it's beautiful up in the high country.

Ah, I wouldn't be climbing any mountain if it weren't for what I have in my brown bag. It's no secret, for any climber with any sense has a pair. Here's one half of my pair, my climbing boot. Not having this boot would have meant slipping and sliding with every step, and it would have taken twice as long to climb to the top in order to peek over.

This special boot helps me because it has a rough sole and heel. Take a look. See the roughness? That gives me a good grip.

It occurred to me after I had reached the top that this is what we need every day. Yes, we need a good grip when the going gets rough and tough. We need to have the courage and the will to keep on going when it isn't easy.

So, here's my advice to you. When you have to do a difficult task, don't give up. This may be learning how to throw a ball straight, learning how to read faster, or learning how to draw better. Get a better grip by saying, "I'll do this yet!"

Or, again, when you fail in doing what you should have done and you have a new chance, get another grip by saying, "This time I'll do it right!"

When I climb Pikes Peak, there are some words from the Bible I keep saying to myself, "Run with perseverance." The only difference is that I say "climb" instead of "run." Perseverance means to keep on doing what needs to be done. It means "Hang in there!" That's what I want you to get a grip on—DON'T GIVE UP, KEEP GOING!

You know, that's what God is saying to us about doing what is right and good and important.

Let us pray.

Dear God: Encourage us to hang in there when the going gets rough and tough. Amen.

No. 26

Sign Here for Freedom

How many of you have heard of the Declaration of Independence? Some of you have talked about it at school.

I have a copy of it in my brown bag. Look at the fancy writing. The original document is in Washington, D.C. It's very, very old, written over two hundred years ago by Thomas Jefferson and adopted by the Continental Congress. The date was July 4, 1776. It was written to tell the world that the United States of America wanted its freedom from England.

Here are some of the things it says: All persons are created equal. That doesn't mean we all have the same talents, such as playing the piano well or kicking a ball the same distance. Rather, it means that God values each of us equally.

Then it states that we have some God-given rights that cannot and should not be taken away from us. For example, there is the right of "Life." This means we can protect ourselves against those who would try to hurt us.

Another right is that of "Liberty." This means we can worship whenever and however we want to, criticize our government if we feel we need to, and work to protect our freedom.

And then there is a third right: "the pursuit of Happiness." This means we have the freedom to do what makes us happy, so long as it doesn't interfere with someone else's freedom to be happy.

Again, these rights are: "Life, Liberty, and the pursuit of Happiness."

I agree, don't you?

Oh, there is a lot more in the Declaration of Independence. There are complaints about how England had been treating us. Then it states that because all attempts had failed to correct these difficulties, the only thing to do was to separate ourselves from England's rule over us and become an independent nation. We did this, but only after this document had been signed and we had fought a war to gain our independence.

The main thing to remember about the Declaration of Independence is that it affirms what God wants for us: freedom. In the Bible it says, "If you can gain your freedom, avail yourself of the opportunity." This is what those signers of this document believed God was calling them to do.

Aren't we asked to do the same today—to speak up for freedom as being what God wants for all people everywhere?

Tomorrow is the Fourth of July, the day we'll remember the signing of the Declaration of Independence. There were fifty-six people who first signed it. See their names? And look at this big signature. That's John Hancock's. He boldly said he was going to sign so the king of England could plainly see it.

Since we believe in freedom and tomorrow is a historic day, how many of you would like to sign this copy of the Declaration of Independence? Good! Sign here for freedom.

Let us pray.

Dear God: Thank you for the gift of freedom. Amen.

No. 27

A Helping Hand

Sara, there's an itch right here in the middle of my back. I would like to scratch it, but I can't. My arm isn't long enough. I can almost get to it, but not quite. Would you help me? Ah . . .! There! Just right! Thank you, thank you.

I guess I could have done it myself. "How?" you ask. I could have reached into my brown bag and pulled this out—a back-scratcher. Have you ever seen one of these? With this plastic hand on the end of this long handle, I could take care of that itch in the middle of my back. Here, let me show you how it works. Ah! That feels good! I have more of an itch back there than I first thought. Excuse me a moment while I do it again. Ahhhhhhh!

You know, this back-scratcher is like a helping hand that goes beyond my own reach. As I do this, the thought occurs to me that there are many, many times in the lives of each of us when we can't do for ourselves what needs to be done. We need help.

For example, when we are sick and it's more than just a simple little cold—something far more serious, like pneumonia—that's when we need someone to help us. So we call a doctor.

Or let's say we're trying to do a math problem and we can't figure it out—that's when we need the help of a good math-minded friend.

Or whenever we need to go where we've never

been before—that's when we need someone to give us directions.

Or if our arms are full of books and we need to have a door opened—that's when we need a helping hand.

Do you get the idea? Sometimes we just can't do what we want to do for ourselves, and we need someone else to do it for us. It's as simple as that.

Let's turn it around. Sometimes we're like this back-scratcher when it comes to someone else. There is always someone who needs the help we can give. We may be able to help a sick person (even though we're not a doctor), assist a mathematically puzzled person, guide a lost person, or open a door for a person whose arms are full.

That's what our religion teaches us—to help one another. It says in the Bible—and this is for all of us to hear—"And let our people learn to apply themselves to good deeds, so as to help cases of urgent need."

When we do this, we're like this back-scratcher. We can do for others what they can't do for themselves.

How do we do this? With love!

Let us pray.

Dear God: For helping hands—ours and others—we are grateful. Amen.

No. 28

Leave Me Alone!

How many of you have a plant at home? Is it just yours and yours alone, a plant for which you are responsible? What kind is it? Do you give it tender, loving care? Good!

In my brown bag I have a plant. It doesn't belong to me, it belongs to my daughter, Suzanne. She bought it yesterday at a plant store, and she has given me permission to show it to you.

What kind of plant is this? A cactus, of course. There are many different kinds of cacti, and this kind is called Golden Barrel. I like the way it looks.

How does this plant differ from other plants? Yes, aside from living mainly in a desert area (or at least in very dry places), the cactus can go a long time without water, and it has these little needles. As you can see, there are many, many needles on this cactus. More than once I've had the bad dream of falling into a bed of cacti and getting stuck by a whole lot of these sharp little needles. And I can remember a few times when I did fall backward on a cactus, much to my sorrow. Has this ever happened to you? It hurts!

The salesperson told Suzanne that these needles are for protection. If one were to break off, a new one would grow in its place. You see, the cactus plant needs to be able to defend itself from some animals that like to eat cacti. If it loses its needles, it can't protect itself. So, God made it possible for the cactus plant to replace its needles when they get broken or fall out for some reason. While it's not the same, it's a bit like growing new teeth when your baby teeth fall out.

I thought of it yesterday as I was holding this cactus plant—oh, not by the needles, but by the pot in which it's planted—how it's like you and me, some of the time. How often have we heard ourselves say that we don't want to be bothered? And our words of warning are like these needles, telling everyone around us:

"Don't touch me!"
"Don't hurt me!"
"Keep away!"
"Back off!"
"Mind your own business!"
"Leave me alone!"

Whatever our reason for saying this—whether it's to a brother or sister, to a classmate at school, to someone here at church, or to a friend up the block—we hope the other person will understand and do as we request.

But, suppose others say the same to us. Do we show understanding (or at least try to understand) and back off and leave them alone as requested? Oh, sure, we may not understand them fully. However, it's very important that we show respect for their feelings. We may wish we could help them in some way. And we do help them by respecting their wish to be left alone. Maybe later they will allow us to do even more for them.

In the Bible it talks about being "respectful in every way," and then it goes on to say, "This is good, and it is acceptable in the sight of God."

Let us pray.
Dear God: Allow us to understand the feelings of others, and show loving respect for them. Amen.

66

No. 29

Sun and Son

Two words. Both start with s. Both sound alike. You know these words, for you use them often. But let me tell you more about them, for when you say one, it sounds like you're saying the other.

I've put them on a big poster, and that's what you see rolled up and sticking out of my brown bag. One of the words is on this side of the poster and the other is on the reverse side.

The first word is SUN.

By the way, do you like my artwork? Does this look like a sun? A modern sun?

Have you ever stopped to think about the sun? It's about ninety-three million miles from us. That's a long way off! But that is where God wants it to be. If it were any closer, we would burn up. And if it were farther away, we would freeze. Yes, God knows what is best for us. When the earth and the sun were first made, God knew just how far apart they should be for our safety and well-being.

We need warmth if we are to live, and that is what the sun gives us. Now, we don't have all the answers about how the sun works, but God does. For us it is that big, bright furnace in the sky that not only gives us light by which to see but also heat to keep us warm. Ah, even more than this, our sun tells of God's love.

Did you ever think of it that way? God gives us

heat and light, two things we need in our world. The giving of these necessities must be viewed as an act of love. In your prayers, thank God for the sun.

On the other side of this poster is that other word which sounds like sun, but it's spelled with an *o* instead of a *u*: SON.

Tell me what this word means. Very good! Here in the church it means we are talking about Jesus. Jesus is God's Son. That's our way of saying that Jesus is very special to God. And Jesus is also very special to us.

This Son of God helps us to feel the warmth of God's love and to see how best to live. The warmth and light of this great love means that God is near to us, loving us here and everywhere.

In the Bible it's said so well: "Jesus is the Son of God. . . . So we know and believe the love God has for us."

When you say your prayers tonight, give thanks to God for this special SON.

The other day I saw a sticker on the bumper of a car that said, "Let the SON shine in." There's that word again, and it's spelled with an *o*. This is a way of saying that we should allow Jesus to come into our lives and let him show us the way God wants us to live. And when we do that, God is part of our lives.

Yes, two words that sound alike: "sun" and "Son." They both help us to know God's love.

Let us pray.

Dear God: Thank you for the ways you make your love known to us, especially for the warm sun and your Son, Jesus. Amen.

No. 30

Those Tacks

At our house we had a problem, and I'm the one who caused it. In fact, I'm somewhat embarrassed to talk about it. But you're my friends, and I feel I can share it with you, knowing that you will understand.

It started a couple of weeks ago. You see, I'm the handyman around the house, and I was repairing the screened top of my compost box. This is the box (four feet by eight feet) in which I put dry leaves, grass cuttings, and leftovers from the table, keeping them there until I can plow them under in my garden. That helps my garden grow better. Anyway, the screen top needed repairing because the old screen had come loose. I didn't have room to fix it in the garage, so I laid it down in the driveway.

Here is where I made my mistake. As I took off the old screen wire, the tiny nails, called tacks, came off in a way I didn't expect. Some of them came off before I could pull them out, flipping in several directions.

Let me show you the size of the tack I'm talking about. Such a small tack deserves a very small bag.

There. And I might add that these tiny tacks have very sharp points. My driveway is concrete, with a few cracks here and there. After I finished, I picked up all the tacks—or at least I thought I had picked them all up. At the time, I didn't think any more about it.

Then things began to happen. First, my son got a flat on the front tire of his bike. Then my daughter reported that the same happened to the back tire of her bike. We had those tires fixed, only to find that the boy across the street and another boy down the street had flat tires on their bikes. I became concerned when I learned that some of my tiny tacks had been found in their tires. In the meantime—in nothing flat—we had two more flats in our family.

Was I angry with myself! I was the cause of all this. What was I to do? Tell me, what do you think I should have done?

Well, I did two things. First, I swept my driveway, trying to pick up any more tacks that might still be there. And I didn't just sweep it with a broom. I took our vacuum sweeper out there and carefully went over every inch of the driveway where I had worked on that screen door.

Finally, I promised to fix all those tires flattened by my tacks. I'm happy to report that all such tires have been fixed.

Why did I do this? Long ago in church school I learned the Golden Rule. It goes something like this: "Do unto others as you would have them do unto you." If people carelessly left tacks where I was riding my bike—if I had a bike—I would want them to fix my punctured tire. If that is what I would want them to do for me, then I should be willing to do the same for them.

Let us pray.
Dear God: We want to do unto others as we would have them do unto us. Amen.

No. 31

Food for Thought

How many of you ate breakfast this morning? Good! Breakfast is one of our most important meals. We need it to get a good start on the day. Our bodies need the energy we get from a good breakfast.

What did you have to eat? Sounds good! May I have breakfast at your house next Sunday?

Really, though, I have a good breakfast every Sunday at my house, and every other morning of the week. I'm a cereal person. Oh, once in a while I'll have bacon and eggs, or maybe pancakes, but most often I eat cereal. There are many different kinds of cereal on our pantry shelf. One is the kind I have in my brown bag this morning.

Cheerios. How many of you eat this kind? Cheerios have been around for a long, long time. I could have brought any number of different cereal boxes. This one just happens to be empty, and that makes it easier to bring, because I don't have to worry about spilling the contents.

Have you ever looked at the cereal box you put in front of your bowl at breakfast? Sure you have. Most boxes have prizes pictured on the outside. The prizes are pictured so that you will buy the cereal. If the rules at your house are like ours, you can't have

71

the prize until you eat down to it. But really, that isn't what I have in mind. Here, let me show you.

Look at this Cheerios box. Yes, there is a prize, which happens to be sugarless gum. But look again—this time at the side of the box—where it tells you what is inside. What is supposed to make this cereal so good for you is listed here for you to read: oat flour, wheat starch, salt, sugar, iron, plus a lot of things that are referred to with big words, such as calcium carbonate and trisodium phosphate. To know what those are, I'd have to get a dictionary. Also, there are many different vitamins mentioned, like C, A, B, B_1, B_6, B_{12}, and D_2.

I tell you all this because it is important to know what you are eating. What you eat becomes you, or—I've heard it said—"You become what you eat." That's true. For example, if you eat too much sugar, your teeth suffer with too many cavities, and you tend to become chubby. Without enough milk or calcium, your bones aren't as strong as they should be. That's why your parents are concerned about your eating habits.

God also wants us to take good care of our bodies, and what we eat is one way of doing that.

The same is true for the other things we put into our lives. For example, bad thoughts have a way of causing more bad thoughts. The same is true about how we act. If we act angry, mean, hard to get along with, moody, grouchy—that is the way we'll become. In like manner, if we become lazy, if we have that "I don't care" kind of attitude, or if we do whatever we want to do whenever we want to do it, then that is going to be us. So it's important to look carefully at what we put into our lives, for that will affect what we will become.

That is why we talk so much at church about love, about being kind and understanding, patient and forgiving, helpful and caring, whether we are at home, at church, at school.

God wants us to put all that love into our lives.

So put that into your bowl and eat it. It's food for thought and action.

Let us pray.

Dear God: Help us to put into our lives what is best for us. Amen.

No. 32

Rings of Life

Last Monday was a sad day at our house. We lost a friend. I suppose you can call a tree a friend, and our friend was the big elm tree on the south side of our house.

It became sick. The city forester came at our request to take a look at it, and she thought it had Dutch elm disease as well as some other problems. Oh, it still had many green leaves, for the disease hadn't yet affected the leaves. The top of the tree looked OK. It was the trunk that caused us concern, for the bark was falling off.

Bark is very important to a tree. It carries the water and food from the roots up to the leaves, and it also carries the warmth of the sun down to the roots. If that doesn't happen, the tree will die. So, we were concerned when the bark began to peel away in big hunks.

The forester was right to say, "That tree must go—this week!" You see, the little beetle that had caused our tree to get sick could have decided to fly over to one of our other elm trees or to our neighbor's elms and make them sick. Once the beetle gets into the tree, there isn't much that can be done. So we did as requested.

Down it came, and that was sad. A friend—Mr. Peterson, Amy's father—came over to help me cut it down. First came the limbs, then the trunk, and then it was hauled off to the dump.

74

But that tree lived a good life. How do I know? I have the proof in my brown bag. Here is a section of the trunk, and the growth rings tell me the tree had a good life. Take a look.

Every year a tree grows a layer of wood, and that is what makes a ring. By counting the rings on this piece of trunk, we can tell that this tree was ten years old. Count them with me. A wide ring tells me that it had a lot of moisture and sunshine that year. Also, we can tell that this tree had good posture, for it stood straight and tall. If it had been slightly bent, as some trees are, the rings would have been wider on one side than on the other.

A tree expert could look at this sawed-off piece of trunk and be able to tell so much more about the life of this tree. But I know it had a good life by the width of each ring.

The rings on this tree tell me that it was older than many of you. But I can see that I was born many years before this tree began to grow. Of course, you can't tell *your* age as this tree does; you have to use a calendar instead. But looking at these rings can cause you—and me—to ask: How is my life going? Are we having good years? Is the sunshine of God's love and care getting through to us, helping us to grow each year as we should?

Granted, we're not like this tree. But God wants us to grow strong and healthy, which means we need to take good care of our bodies. Also, God wants us to grow wise in our thoughts, which means learning how to use our minds so that we can think well. And certainly we're to grow in our faith, which means we need to trust more and more in God.

Let us pray.
Dear God: May we grow in ways that are pleasing to you. Amen.

No. 33

Let Me See

Why are you looking at me that way? You say there is something about me that looks different? But what is that something? Right, I don't have my glasses on. Have any of you seen them? I had them on earlier. Maybe they're in my brown bag. They are!

Of course, I'm just having fun with you—just teasing. I put my glasses in my bag just before sitting down with you.

How many of you wear glasses? How long have you been wearing yours? I first started wearing mine when I was about eighteen. One day I noticed that I couldn't see very well what the teacher was writing on the chalkboard. It was blurry. When I moved closer, I knew what was wrong. So I went to the eye doctor, and he told me I needed glasses. Ever since, I've had to wear them if I want to see things clearly.

But it's not my intention this morning to give you the medical history of my eyes. Rather, I want to talk with you about a problem I have with my glasses (and I'm not talking about them sliding down my nose, like this). The problem is my glasses are always getting dirty.

Sure, I clean them. But they get dirty so quickly! Where all the dirt comes from is a mystery to me. Oh, it's not a total mystery, for some of it is dust from the air, fingerprint smudges, and spatterings of this and that. It's a problem. Do you have this problem?

As I was cleaning my glasses the other day, the thought occurred to me that it's very important for us to see the world as it really is. The biggest problem we have in seeing as clearly as we should comes from how we smudge up our own view. Selfishness is another way of referring to this. Our selfishness keeps us from seeing other people as we should.

Let's say something good has happened to a friend of yours—like getting a new swing set—and instead of being happy for your friend, you're sad and angry because you still have an old swing set. Your view of your friend's happiness is somewhat blocked because you are thinking too much about yourself.

Or, let's say your mom or dad wants to go downtown to run an errand and you're too young to stay home by yourself. Instead of willingly going with them, you throw a temper tantrum and act ugly. That's when you can't see beyond yourself because of the smudges of selfishness.

Again, you may brag and brag that you're the better runner, that you have the best clothes, and that you get to do more things than your friend does. How does that make your friend feel? Not good! What you say may be true, but your bragging is selfish, keeping you from seeing how your words hurt.

Jesus said, "Having eyes do you not see?"

Hey, I need to clean my glasses—but you know I'm talking about more than just dirt on the lenses.

Let us pray.

Dear God: May we not smudge up our view with selfishness. Amen.

No. 34

As Others See Us

L ast Sunday we talked about eyeglasses.
Remember? This morning I have another pair, but
they're different from the regular kind of eyeglasses.
Let me show you. Sunglasses!

How many of you have a pair of sunglasses? Ah,
several of you do. Sunglasses are very useful. They
protect our eyes from the sun. The dark glass cuts
down on the glare that causes us to squint.

There are different kinds we can buy. For
example, now they have eyeglasses that will turn dark
when we are out in the sun, and then when we come
back indoors they become clear like regular
eyeglasses. (Don't ask me how they work, for I really
don't know, except to say it is special glass.) Also,
there are sunglasses that we can clip onto our regular
glasses, one set of glasses on top of another set. And
then there's the half-and-half kind—dark at the top
and lighter toward the bottom.

Ah, looking in my brown bag I see another kind
of sunglasses. Let me try these on and see what you
think. What's the difference? Right, it looks like I put
two mirrors in front of my eyes. By looking at me you
see yourself.

This pair is made to reflect the light. On one side
it looks like a mirror, and on the other side it's just
darkened glass. Let me take them off and show you
the other side. Don't ask me how these work, for I
would have to say the same as I said about those
other sunglasses, "I don't know—special glass."

78

Surely you've seen people wear this kind of
sunglasses. I have, especially up on the ski slopes.
You see, the snow really reflects the light of the sun,
and this makes it even harder to see. These special
mirror sunglasses bounce the bright glare away from
our eyes, thus allowing us to see better.

But I didn't bring these mirror sunglasses just to
talk about how they help skiers or any other person
wearing them on a very bright day. I'm amazed that I
see myself when I look at someone wearing them. Of
course, I know I am only seeing myself in the mirrors
of these glasses. Yet, I keep thinking of how I look in
the eyes of that person.

There was a poet who lived a long time ago by
the name of Robert Burns, and he wrote something
I've often remembered. It comes from the poem
entitled "To a Louse."

O wad some Power the giftie gie us
To see oursels as ithers see us!

That makes me stop and think! If I really knew how
others saw me, I would learn a few things about
myself, and I might want to make some changes in
myself. Some hard questions would have to be asked,
like: Do they see me as loving? as honest? as patient?
as friendly? as helpful? as nice? as fair? as happy? as
kind? Or, do they see me in other ways, which aren't
so good?

We can't really see through other people's eyes,
but we can learn a lot about ourselves from others.
Then we can do as it says in the Bible, and learn
"not to think of [ourselves] more highly than [we]
ought to think, but to think with sober judgment."

Let us pray.
Dear God: Help us see the truth about ourselves
as others see it. Amen.

No. 35

Ants

This is a special weekend. For many of you it is special because this is the last weekend before you must go back to school. For all of us, it is a national holiday called "Labor Day."

In my brown bag I have a gallon jar of dirt. You may ask, "What's so special about that?" Well, if you will look closer, you'll see that there is more in this jar than just dirt. Do you see the ants? This is my ant farm.

Several days ago I put this ant farm together. It was easy. In fact, you may want to make one. All it takes is a big jar like this, some good soil, and some ants. This isn't the first time I've done this, for when I was your age, I did it many times. After filling the jar with dirt, I found a big anthill. These are the big, brownish-red kind of ants. Very carefully I put a stick down where they could climb on it, and then I quickly put them in the jar, shaking them off the stick. I tried to count how many I put in here, but I was forced to work too fast to keep an accurate count. I didn't want to get too many, for that would make them too crowded.

Look at how busy they have been! They have tunneled down in the jar along the sides. It's fun to see them work.

Ants are interesting to watch, especially when they eat. And they love to eat! In here are some bread crumbs and some chocolate cake. Chocolate cake? That's right. That gives them something sweet, which is important. And I have some leaves for them to eat. I understand they like leaves to nibble on; their favorites are leaves from fruit trees. There is also a dead fly in here. After all, they need a little meat in their diet. And every day I give them a few drops of water, for ants get thirsty too.

Watching my ants, I've become convinced that they are very smart. Did you know they have leaders and followers? They also talk to one another. How? They talk with their feelers. I've put my ear to the mouth of the jar, and there is no sound; yet they seem to say things to one another.

They seem to care about one another too. For example, they are always ready to help one another, especially when there is trouble. When they eat, they share. They care for their sick. When an ant dies, there are special "undertaker" ants who will bury it. They are very clean little creatures, for when there is litter they will carry it away. Where? They carry it to what we might call a city dump, a place just for litter and trash.

Although I haven't seen it, I've read from experts who know about insects that ants like wrestling and the game of "keep away" with seeds (maybe that is their form of soccer).

There is much more I could say about ants, but listen to what it says in the Bible, in the book of Proverbs: "Go to the ant, consider her ways, and be wise."

Notice again how these ants are working together. That's what I want you to remember this morning.

We too need to work together at all times. On Labor Day we will not work, for that is when we stop to be happy we have work to do. But when we work, let's help one another do the work that God wants us to do.

Let us pray.
Dear God: May we work together as we do our work for you. Amen.

No. 36

A Rocky Lesson

This past week has been rocky. By this I don't
mean it has been a rough or difficult week. Just
the opposite! It has been a good week. This time,
"rocky" means "good." To prove it, I've brought
three rocks in my brown bag.

The first rock has an interesting history. It came
from deep, deep down in the earth. We call it
volcanic rock. Last Monday our family was traveling
through northeastern New Mexico and stopped at a
national monument called Capulin Mountain. It's an
old, extinct volcano (meaning it's not on fire
anymore). The scientists say the mountain was formed
by a volcano about seven or eight thousand years
ago. At that time this rock, which was deep in the
earth, became very hot. Pressure behind it caused it
to come shooting up through a crack in the earth.
Notice how jagged it is.

The second rock looks like this. You say, "I've
seen rocks like that one." Sure you have. In fact, you
have them right in your backyard or not far from
where you live. This is just an ordinary rock. And
there are millions, billions, trillions, yes, countless
numbers of this kind of rock in our world. We have
some mountains at our doorstep which get their name
from rocks like these. You know, the Rocky
Mountains. Rocks, rocks everywhere!

The third rock is different. It isn't from this world. It's from outer space. Before it got here, it was much larger. But as it neared the earth, much of it burned. This is what is left. We call it a meteorite. Many meteorites have a lot of metal in them, such as iron, but this one has more stone in it than metal. I tested it with a good magnet. Anyway, it came from "out there" somewhere.

Why do I have these three rocks this morning? Because all three are connected. They don't come from the same place—one is from deep within the earth; another is from the surface of the earth; and the last is from out of this world—but all three were made by God. That's the connection. And this tells us that God has created everything. From the center of the earth to the far reaches of space, God has made it all. "In the beginning God created. . . ." And these rocks are part of what was created by God.

When I was up on that volcano this past week, I read over the comments in the visitors' book. One visitor had written: "God, you done good!" And that's the truth!

Let us pray.
Dear God: Thank you for these rocks that have told us about your creation. Amen.

No. 37

It's in the Book

My brown bag is heavy this morning. It's not the bag that is heavy but what's in it. I could keep you guessing, but I won't. It's a book. Here, let me show you.

Have you ever seen a book this big? It's a special book, a dictionary, and a special dictionary at that. This is *Webster's Third New International Dictionary.* A friend gave it to me as a gift. I like it, and so does our new dog. (See where he chewed on the corner of it? That dog is going to be a smart one yet!)

This dictionary is important because it has almost all the words in our English language. There are a few words that aren't in here—special words used in special ways—but this big dictionary has close to half a million words. That's a lot! I didn't count all these words; there's no way I could do that. This information is given on the cover of the book. It takes over 2,750 pages to list all the words with their many meanings.

Well, I'm glad I have this special dictionary, in spite of how much it weighs. In my work I often use a dictionary. This big dictionary will help me even more than the other ones I have.

Answer this question: What do you think the most important word in this dictionary is? Those are some good answers.

The word I think is most important—and a couple of you mentioned it—is found over on page 1340: "love."

What would this world be like if there were no love? Terrible! Horrible! Sad! However, we do have love in our world, and we thank God for that.

In the Bible it says, "God so loved the world. . . ." In many, many ways, we have experienced how God has loved us through parents and friends, through the church, and very much through Jesus. God loves you and me and everyone, and we should never forget this. God is love, and that is what we talk about at church every Sunday, just as we are doing today.

God wants us to become more loving!

Thus, this little word love shouldn't stay in this big book; rather, it must become part of us, part of what we say and part of what we do.

Let us pray.
Dear God: Help us to be more loving. Amen.

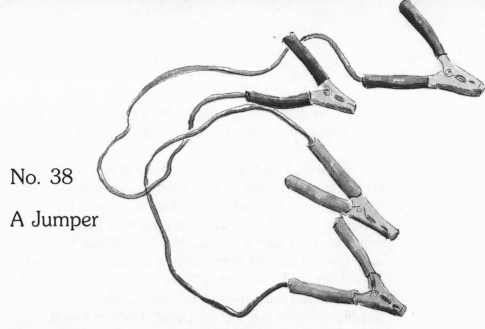

No. 38

A Jumper

I have something in my brown bag. You may or may not know what it is. Let me show you, then you tell me what you think it is. There.

It's a jumper cable.

You may ask, "A what?" This is a special kind of cable that is used to get a car started when the battery has run down. By using this cable to connect another car battery to your car battery, you get enough starting power from the other battery to get the motor going. I ought to know, for it happened to me yesterday.

Yesterday was a good day, although there were a few moments when I began questioning whether it was going to end up that way. You see, I had to go to a meeting in a distant city. This meant driving to Denver in order to fly to Salt Lake City. It was hard getting up at 4:15 A.M. to get ready and to arrive on time at the airport.

The flight was about an hour of smooth flying with no problem in landing or getting to the meeting. As I've said, the day was going great. The same was true on the flight back.

However, at the Denver airport I began to have my doubts. It was then about 6:30 P.M. I tried to start my car and quickly realized I wasn't going anywhere fast. Nothing happened! Absolutely nothing! Do you know what was wrong? Right! My battery was dead. That means the battery wouldn't start the car. There I sat.

What had happened? I glanced at my dashboard, and I saw the problem. I had left my car lights on all day long, for about eleven and a half hours. My battery is a good one, but even the best battery is going to run down if treated like that. It had been dark when I arrived at the airport on my way to Salt Lake City, and, being in a hurry to catch the plane, I simply locked my car—not thinking about the headlights—and ran for the plane. I felt so foolish when I saw what I had done! In fact, I'm rather embarrassed to tell you about it this morning.

There I was, a long way from home and with a car that wouldn't start. What was I to do? My family was going to worry about me if I didn't get home on schedule. And wouldn't you know, I had parked on the top part of the parking lot where there weren't many other cars. Well, as people came from their planes going to their cars, I asked again and again, "Do you have a jumper cable?"

At last, someone had a jumper cable, and that person, even though he seemed to be in a big hurry, saw my difficulty and quickly agreed to help me get my car started. I wish I knew his name and address, for I would like to write him a thank-you letter.

All the way home I kept thinking how wonderful it was of him to stop and help me when I really needed help. I kept saying to myself that if I ever have the opportunity to help someone in need, and I'm able to help, I'm going to do it.

I'm not just thinking about helping someone who has a dead battery. If that is the need or difficulty, I'll do what I can. But there are so many other ways to help, depending on what the problem is.

Furthermore, I want to help as this man did, without drawing attention to myself. Doing it just for the love of doing it is a way of loving others.

Jesus said, "Let your light so shine . . . that they may see your good works and give glory to [God] who is in heaven." Isn't that what loving is all about?

Let us pray.

Dear God: May we always be willing to help others. Amen.

No. 39

Molehills and Mountains

Have you ever seen a molehill?
"A what?" you ask.
A molehill. On this index card I've drawn one with a felt-tip marker. As you can see, it isn't very big.

A molehill is made by a little animal called a mole. It digs its tunnel home just beneath the surface of the ground, and the place it pushes up the dirt for air or for a door to the tunnel is called a molehill. As you can see (as shown by my drawing), it isn't very big.

Have you ever heard the phrase "making a mountain out of a molehill"? In my brown bag I have something that will help to show how a molehill can be made into a mountain. I know this sounds impossible, but look at what happens. When I take this magnifying glass and put it over this molehill I've drawn, it becomes larger. If I try this more powerful magnifying glass, the molehill becomes even larger. In my bag I have a very, very powerful magnifying glass. Let me hold it up to this molehill. WOW! See how big the molehill is now!

Notice that this molehill is only as big as it is on this card. What we have done is make it *seem* bigger than it really is.

We make mountains out of molehills when we make something seem bigger than it really is. No, I'm not talking about magnifying a drawing or even taking a real molehill and somehow making it seem like a real mountain, like Pikes Peak. Let me explain.

A friend of yours might say, "I won't be over to play today," and you could imagine that she means, "I don't WANT to come over and play today." You could make much more out of what your friend said than your friend meant.

Or, you will have a spelling test at school on words that aren't too difficult, but maybe you become nervous and worry about it until it's a much bigger problem than it should be.

Or, one day you break something your parents value. As you wait for them to find out about it, you make it into a bigger concern than your parents would ever consider it to be. (They may be more concerned why you didn't come to them right away and tell them what happened.)

Do you see what I mean? Don't enlarge or magnify a small problem. To avoid this, I remind myself of what it says in the Bible, ". . . rightly handling the word of truth." That is what God wants us to do—keep things down to their proper size.

Let us pray.
Dear God: Help us to keep from making mountains out of molehills. Amen.

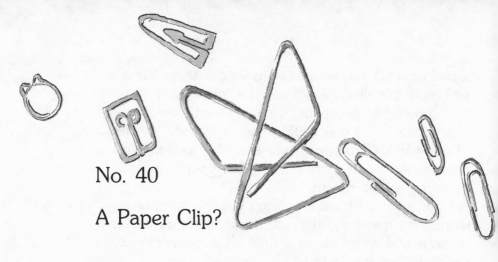

No. 40

A Paper Clip?

In this small bag is something from my desk drawer. I've brought some paper clips.

Do you know what a paper clip is for? It holds together two or more pieces of paper. Really it's nothing more than a piece of wire, bent in a special way.

I couldn't do without paper clips. In my desk drawer I have well over a hundred of them (I counted them last night). Not all of them are of the same shape and size. Some are big, some are small. And I also have some odd-looking ones, like this one with a straight top and crossed wire legs. Then there is another kind, which looks like a box turned in on itself, or this one that is pointed. And here's my favorite kind, the one I use for a bookmark. It's small and round.

Even though I've used paper clips for years, I must confess that I often take them for granted. That means, even though they continue to do their job, I don't give them very much thought.

When I think of a paper clip, I'm reminded of our families. Each of us has a family. A family may have two parents or maybe just one; it may have brothers and sisters or, maybe, grandparents.

You know, our families help us to hold our lives together. They provide us with food, clothing, and shelter, along with companionship, help, comfort, and love. It's easy to take those nearest to us for granted, and not give them much thought or appreciation. We all need to look again at what our families mean to us and be thankful.

Again, what about our community or city? It holds us together in ways that make life easier and happier. Aren't we glad we have good roads on which to drive, good schools in which to learn, and nice parks in which to play? And, of course, your parents help to pay for these things with their taxes. But we take for granted how wonderful this is, until we go to some other city where they don't have what we have here. Oh, we have a lot to be thankful for.

Or, again, there's the church. It helps us to learn more about God and Jesus and how to be more loving. If it didn't teach us this, think about how empty our lives would be. Yes, it's easy to take the church for granted and not see or appreciate all the good it does for us. Let's remember how it holds us together for good and be thankful.

And again, I'm thinking about God. God made this world and us. Whether we realize it or not, whether we take God for granted or not, God holds the world and us together. For this we need to give thanks.

Well, we've come a long way from these little paper clips. But they have helped us to think about what holds us together.

I want to give each of you a paper clip as a reminder of what we've talked about this morning. Clip it on your collar. Let it remind you of all the things that hold us together, and to be thankful.

Let us pray.
Dear God: For paper clips and for so very much more, we are thankful. Amen.

No. 41

A Tape Job

Let me share something with you I read the other
day. I have no idea who wrote this. Whoever it
was should be thanked, for it says a lot.

> Words are such funny things,
> They can be lovely or give bitter stings.
> Think hard before you let them go,
> You cannot get them back, you know.

These lines tell us that we need to be careful how
we use words. They can hurt!

Of course, they can be lovely too. Remember
those times when someone said a kind word to you
about something you had done or how you looked,
and how that made you feel so good on the inside.
After hearing it—if you're like me—you were very
happy, and you wanted to do a better job next time.
Oh, yes, it's great to be praised! And these words are
remembered for a long time.

But what about those times when someone says
something that hurts, such as not liking the way you
do something or not liking the way you dress or not
liking . . . you name it. Those words sting, don't they?
You don't like what they say, even if it is the truth.
Although you don't forget the lovely words, those
hurting words are remembered even longer.

It's very important for us to watch how we use our words, even when they are kind and good and lovely. When they are on the bright side, telling someone something nice, we need to be sure they are true.

However, it's the stinging words that concern me even more. They hurt! And when we give out stinging words, it's usually because we're angry or because someone has said hurtful things to us. And sometimes we're just not careful enough about the feelings of others.

May I make a suggestion? When we're about to say something we'll later regret, we need a tape job. "A what?" Haven't you ever heard someone say, "I ought to tape my mouth shut"?

In my brown bag I have a roll of masking tape, and whenever I'm tempted to say something that shouldn't be said and that might hurt someone, I say to myself, "Jerry, tape your mouth!" Here, let me show you how that would look and what that would sound like.

Mmm, mmm mmm'm mmmmmmmmmmm mmm m'm mmmmmm.

You didn't understand what I said? Good! It was something I shouldn't have said.

No, I'm not saying you should tape your mouth with masking tape. But I am saying that we—you and I—need to watch what we say. Even in the Bible it advises us to be "slow to speak, slow to anger." That means we need to be careful what we say and how we say it, so that it is true and loving and helpful. If what we say is good, then it's pleasing to others as well as to God. If what we say is bad, we need a tape job.

Let us pray.
Dear God: Help us to say it right or not say it at all. Amen.

95

No. 42

Breath of God

Bubbles. Bubbles. Bubbles.
When you hear this word, what do you think of? Bubble gum? Bubble bath? Bubbles in a fizzy pop? Bubbles blown by a goldfish?

Are you familiar with the song that has these words in it?

I'm forever blowing bubbles,
Pretty bubbles in the air.

What I have in my brown bag makes those words just bubble up in my thoughts. Let me show you.

It's a toy bubble-maker. How many of you have one or have had one? It's fun! With this little plastic blower and a good supply of soapy water, you can make bubbles, bubbles, bubbles. They are such pretty, round, little spheres, floating through the air until they silently pop.

There are several ways of creating bubbles. You can run, letting the air push out the bubbles. Or you

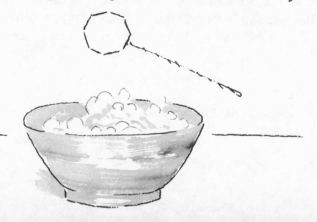

can swing your arm fast, and out they come—not one, not two, but many. I think the best way is to blow them out. Watch.

Blowing bubbles makes me think of God and of us and of life. You see, it's God who gives us life, first when we are born and even now. As it says in the Bible, "The Lord God formed man of dust from the ground, and breathed into his nostrils the breath of life; and man became a living being." (Please don't think the Bible is just talking about doing this for boys. The word man once was used to mean all the people—girls and boys, women and men—all of us.) God's breath of life was given and is still being given in the gentlest of ways.

When I blow on this bubble-maker, I must blow in a gentle way. If I blow too hard, the bubbles will pop. So I do it just right because I care.

God cares even more about the new life that is coming into being than I could ever care about these bubbles. The breath of God has been shared with us all because God loves us.

Does God really breathe? No, not like we do. This is just the way the writer of this part of the Bible tried to talk about God, saying that God wants to give us life, which is what happened when we were born. Even now God wants to make us more alive. I like the way we sing about this in a familiar hymn:

> Breathe on me, Breath of God,
> Fill me with life anew,
> That I may love what thou dost love,
> And do what thou wouldst do.

These bubbles can remind us of what God is doing for us.

Let us pray.
Dear God: Thank you for giving us life. Amen.

No. 43

The Domino Lesson

Dominoes, anyone?

Have you ever played dominoes? A few of you have. Do the rest of you know about this game? Maybe it would be of help if I showed you a domino. I just happen to have one in my brown bag.

As you can see, this domino is small, flat, and long, with some white dots on it. You lay dominoes down end to end and add the dots to score points (like a five or a ten or a fifteen or any larger number that can be divided by five). I won't explain more to you, but if you have a set of dominoes at home, maybe your parents will show you how to play this game. Ask them to play with you.

Let me show you something else you can do with dominoes. I'll just pour out all the dominoes I have in my bag. Give me just a few seconds to set them up and then I'll show you what I have in mind.

Notice that I've set these dominoes on end, lining them up in a row. They are spaced just so—not too far apart and not too close together. How many of you have done this with dominoes? You probably know what I'm going to do next. No, I'm not going to do it, I'm going to ask Greg to do it. Greg, put your finger here and gently push. And down they all go, one after another. Do you want to see that again? OK, let me set them up again. Amy, this time *you* push the end domino.

Wasn't that fun! And we only had nineteen. Think what it would be like if we had a hundred. The other evening on the news I saw a man set up about ten thousand dominoes and do this—and was that fun to watch!

They all fell down, because each one had an effect on the other. The first one fell into the second one, causing it to fall into the third one, causing the others to do the same as each fell into the next one in the row. That tells me something about influence.

Influence? It's how we affect others. We all have an influence on someone. That person then reacts in a way that influences another person. And it continues on and on. I call it the "domino lesson."

How are we influencing others? Is it for the good or for the bad? Do we make others feel better or worse? Are they more loving because we're more loving, or are they grouchy and difficult because that's the way we are? You know, how we are and how we act affects others. Our behavior starts a domino kind of action and affects more people than we might think when all is said and done. When the action starts with us, we need to ask ourselves, "What are we starting?"

If it's a bad influence, I would hope we would stop it and not pass it on to others. If it's a good influence, I would hope we would pass it on.

Yes, every day each of us will have an effect on someone. Let it be a good effect, and then may it get passed on and on and on.

Let us pray.
Dear God: Help us be a good influence on others. Amen.

No. 44

Binoculars and the Bible

Excuse me a moment. I want to check something out.

What are these things I'm holding up to my eyes? Right. Binoculars. Recently, I received this pair as a gift from my parents, and I'm really excited about having binoculars. It's something I've always wanted. That's why I've bagged them up this morning and brought them to church.

But if you don't mind, for just a moment or two I want to check something out with them. I'm looking at our big stained-glass window, and these binoculars make it seem as if I could reach out and touch the glass. The glass is so pretty with the sun shining through it. I've always been interested in how the stained glass is put together with those strips of lead. Now I can take a close look. Also, I see some dirt up there, and there is that cobweb we've talked about before (although I don't see Mrs. Spider at home).

The other day I was looking at the mountains with these binoculars, and it made me feel cold, for the snow up there seemed so very, very near. And I love to look at the stars and the moon with this viewing aid, for it makes them so much closer.

Do you know how binoculars work? I'm not going to take this pair apart. Knowing how I fix things, I may not get all the parts back in their proper places. In here there are special kinds of glass, called lenses, which make things seem nearer. Of course, when something is closer, it seems larger. That window up there seems as if it's right in front of me.

How many of you have ever looked through a pair of binoculars? You know what I'm talking about. Oh, I wish we had time now for everybody to take a look, but we don't. After church I'll be happy to let you look through my binoculars.

Making things that are far away seem close up—isn't that what we're trying to do here at church? Here I'm thinking not only about a long distance but also about a faraway time.

Often we think of God as way up there, somewhere in space. We ask, "How can we make God seem closer to us?" Also, Jesus lived a long time ago—about two thousand years ago. That seems far off to us, and it is hard to see with our mind's eye. To see Jesus close up, we need help.

Do you think we can see them better with these binoculars? Of course not! What a funny question that is! And yet, how can we have both God and Jesus seem closer to us?

My bag isn't empty. What I have in there is my Bible. This pair of binoculars caused me to think of my Bible, for it helps me—when I read it and understand what it's saying—to realize how close God and Jesus seem to me. In fact, it says that God and Jesus are very close and very near to me—and to you.

101

The difference between this pair of binoculars and the Bible is that when you lay the binoculars down, the thing you've been looking at is still far off. When you lay the Bible down, having read and understood it, you know that God and Jesus are near, very near, to you.

Let us pray.
Dear God: We are thankful for the Bible, for it shows us how near you and Jesus really are to us. Amen.

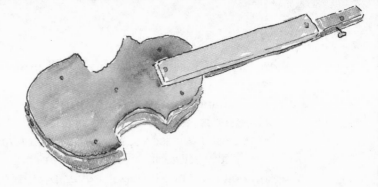

No. 45

More Than Just Fiddling Around

May I show you something that is very precious to me? It's in my brown bag, and it's one of the pride and joys of my youth. A violin!

I made this violin. Really! I was about nine years old then. You see, I wanted to learn to play the violin, and I didn't have one. Oh, I wanted one more than anything, but no one thought I was serious. When I asked for a violin, the answer was, "Oh, you're too young for that. Wait awhile."

I wasn't easily discouraged. I decided to make a violin—this one. It's not the best violin I've ever seen, but when I was nine it seemed the best ever.

I can still remember making it. For the front and the back I used some old hardboard I found in the barn, and once I had cut two pieces in the shape of a violin I nailed them together with a piece of wood in between, sandwich-like. Then I whittled a piece of wood for the neck to which I nailed a long, thin piece of wood for the fingering board. Four strings were then stretched on it, held tight by big thumbtacks.

As for the bow that goes with it, I don't have it, but I wish I did. I can remember making it. It was a long stick with a nail at each end. For the horsehair (all violin bows have horsehair), I vividly recall going with scissors in hand and cutting off some of the horse's tail. (I wonder if Dad knew I was doing this?) Then, I tied these hairs on both nails, and I had a bow.

What about the sound? Well, it wasn't much to listen to! But that didn't bother me.

Making this violin convinced my parents of my seriousness, for soon I was given a real violin, and I began taking lessons. However, that's another story.

In the Bible it says, "Endurance produces character." That thought never occurred to me then, but it has crossed my mind since. It means that you're a better person if you learn to finish what you start—provided it's worth finishing. With me it was wanting a violin to play. I was determined, even if I had to make my own violin, which you can see I did.

Don't give up if there is something you really want to do and it's worth doing. Keep working at it! Even though it may take time and some people may say you should spend your time doing something else, don't give up. You'll be a better person for sticking to it until the task is done. That's what is meant by character. Sure, there is a lot more meant by this big word "character," but it's important that you learn the lesson of keeping yourself going until you've done what you need to do.

Look at it this way: Are you happy with yourself when you don't finish what you feel you should finish? Of course not!

Think often about these words from the Bible, and remember what we've talked about this morning: "Endurance produces character." Then, get on with it.

Let us pray.

Dear God: When we have something important to do, remind us not to give up. Amen.

No. 46

A Waste of Talent

Last Sunday I showed you the violin I made when I was about nine years old. Do you remember why I made it? Right. Because I wanted to learn how to play the violin and I didn't have one.

Well, after my parents saw what I had made, they decided to get me a real violin and have me take lessons from Professor Lloyd. He was the orchestra and band leader at the high school.

You've never seen anyone happier than I was, or anyone prouder of an instrument. I can still remember holding my new violin in my hands when I first got it and then looking at it for the longest time. After I looked at every inch of it (oh, it was beautiful!), Mother helped me tune the strings and tighten the bow. She played the right notes on the piano (E, A, D, G), and I twisted those little pegs at the end of the violin until I thought it sounded like the notes on the piano. After doing this, I put it under my chin and tried to play. It didn't sound very good; it was very screechy and scratchy. But that didn't bother me! I was at last playing a real violin.

If I may say so, I became a fair violinist. I was chosen to be the first chair in the junior high orchestra. But then I quit.

There are two reasons why I quit. The first is because I wanted to play football, and I foolishly thought a football player didn't have time to play the violin. Second, I was tired of practicing.

Do I still play? Here, let me show you how well I play. I have my violin in my brown bag (oh, yes, I've kept it all these years). I would like to play for you the one piece I remember, "Twinkle, Twinkle, Little Star."

Why did you cover your ears?

It's sad, but I've really forgotten how to play the violin. To this day I'm sorry I quit.

But something else needs to be said about my violin-playing. You see, I didn't use a talent God gave me. Do you know what the word talent means? The dictionary gives several meanings, but I like the one that says talent is a natural ability to do something.

Yes, I feel I was given the ability to play the violin. I seriously doubt that I would have ever become a great violinist, because I wasn't that talented, nor did I like practicing all that much (it takes a lot of practicing to become great or even very good). However, I could have learned even more about the violin, enough to have really enjoyed playing for the rest of my life. That didn't happen, because I didn't take advantage of the talent God gave me.

Oh, we all have God-given talents, whether it's to play a musical instrument, to play ball, to act, to grow plants, or to help others—the list is long. These kinds of talents are gifts for us to use and not neglect. The Bible says, "Do not neglect the gift you have." And then in the very next sentence, it says, "Practice . . . so that all may see your progress." We're to use the talents God gives us.

Let us pray.

Dear God: Help us to use the talents you have given us. Amen.

No. 47

Pass the Pretzels

When you think of Thanksgiving, what comes to mind?

Pilgrims. Yes!
Food. For sure!
No school. OK!
Family. Right!
Church service. Certainly!
God. Absolutely!

All these go together to make Thanksgiving Day special.

Let's talk about food, for that seems to be the way we most often express our thankfulness—by eating together. And what do we usually eat on Thanksgiving Day?

Turkey. Yes!
Stuffing. For sure!
Sweet potatoes. OK!
Gravy. Right!
Cranberries. Certainly!
Pumpkin pie. Absolutely!

Plus, there's a lot more. In fact, there is so much to eat that we usually eat too much and think we'll never ever want to eat again. But, of course, we will. The Pilgrims ate most of those special foods we eat today. That's why we eat turkey every year and why we sometimes call this special day "Turkey Day."

Have you ever eaten pretzels on Thanksgiving Day? Pretzels? Let's take one from my brown bag.

A pretzel is good to eat. As you can see, it's brittle and twisted, glazed and salted. Pretzels were first made by monks in southern France as a reward for those children who learned to say their prayers. The first ones were made from twisted leftover dough. The monks noticed that this twist looked like the crossed arms of a child praying. So they started making them and giving them to the children as a reward for saying their prayers. The word pretzel means "small reward."

Why do we talk about pretzels at Thanksgiving time? When we eat our big meal and when we eat the leftovers, it's important for us to bow our heads and prayerfully tell God how thankful we are for all the many blessings we have.

Each time we look at a pretzel—now that we've talked about it—let's remember to say our prayers, our prayers of thanks.

Yes, I'm asking you to start a new tradition by having an unusual food on your Thanksgiving Day table—pretzels—along with everything else. How about it?

Since today and every day should be a day when we prayerfully tell God how thankful we are, I want to give you a pretzel now. My brown bag is full of pretzels, one for each of you. Take one (you can eat it now), and when you get home, tell your parents what we talked about this morning. Then they will understand when you ask for pretzels this Thanksgiving Day.

Let us pray.
Dear God: Accept our prayers of thanks. Amen.

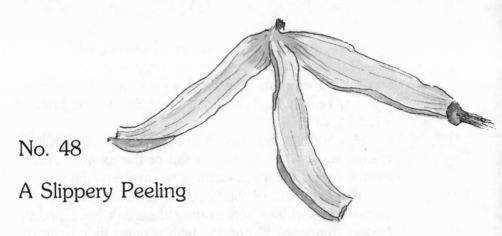

No. 48

A Slippery Peeling

I ate it for breakfast this morning. And what I didn't eat, I brought in my brown bag. No, what is in my bag is not something to eat. That sounds confusing, doesn't it? It's a banana peel. The garbage would be a better place for it, but before we toss it, let's talk about it.

Have you ever seen someone slip on a banana peel? That's right, they fall down! Have you ever slipped on one? It wasn't funny, was it? It hurts! But for a long time people have been laughing at the thought of others slipping on banana peels, except when it happens to them.

By the way, this moist lining is what makes the banana peel slippery. See?

I brought this peel because it reminds me of a slip I made last week. No, I didn't slip and fall on it. Rather, I slipped in something I said. It's what is called "a slip of the tongue," and this banana peel reminds me of that. Do you remember what I said wrong?

This: "Now that Thanksgiving is over, Easter is just a few weeks away." Wow! I meant to say Christmas! And I didn't realize I had said this until after the worship service when I was told of my mistake.

We all make this kind of slip. We say what we don't mean to say. It just comes out wrong. At times we may realize our error and quickly correct ourselves. At other times we go on talking, not realizing what we've said wrong, only to have someone correct us later. When I was told about my slip, my reply was, "Did I say that? Surely you knew what I meant."

A good listener tries to understand what is really meant, even when there is a slip of the tongue. This means caring for that person with understanding.

Another kind of slip happens for those who say something and later realize they shouldn't have said it. Maybe they spoke in anger, with a hasty judgment, or because of some misinformation, and later they regret what they said. This too may be considered a slip of the tongue. What we do then is the same. We try our best to understand and try to get behind the words spoken in order to hear what is really meant.

Jesus said, "Hear and understand." He was saying that it's not what a person says that matters as much as what is meant. Being understanding is the loving thing to do.

Let us pray.

Dear God: Help us to hear and understand what others are really saying. Amen.

No. 49

Those Little Gifts

" 'Twas the night before Christmas, when
all through the house
    Not a creature was stirring, not even a
mouse. . . . "

You know that poem! In the last few weeks, how
many times have you heard it?

I like this poem because it was one of the first
poems I can remember hearing. Don't ask me how
old I was then, but I was very young. It was written
over a hundred years ago by a minister named
Clement C. Moore, who wrote it for his children.
Others heard about it, and after hearing it read, they
told others. It's lasted a long time and is still a favorite
at this time of year.

We have a few weeks before we get to that
special night, but there is one line in this poem that
speaks of what I have in my brown bag. Care to
guess? Let me quote it, and then you'll know: "The
stockings were hung by the chimney with care."

Here's my stocking! Sure, I put my stocking up
every year. Don't you? It has my name on it. Every
member of our family has a stocking, and on
Christmas Eve we will hang them by the chimney with
care.

It happens every Christmas morning. I get so
excited about the gifts under the tree that I forget to
look in my stocking. Then I'm asked, "Well, what did

111

you get in your stocking?" And I have to admit, "Oh, I forgot to look!"

It's so easy to overlook the small gifts. Yet just because they're small doesn't mean they're less important than the big gifts. Consider what I had in my stocking last year—yes, I still remember. There were pencils, and I dearly love pencils. Every Christmas I get pencils, which I appreciate. There was also a special little pencil sharpener, which I keep in my desk drawer. Then, there were other little thoughtful gifts in my stocking: a new toothbrush, a new razor, some paper clips, and my favorite kind of candy. All these little gifts I wanted and needed. How thoughtful!

This causes me to think about all those other little gifts of thoughtfulness in everyday life that aren't given the notice they deserve. For example, a smile—especially when it's easier to frown. Or, what about two of the nicest words in the English language: "Thank you"? Or, what about a helping hand, a kind word, or a loving touch? These aren't considered big gifts, costing a lot of money, but, oh, how special they are.

As we receive, let's remember how to receive. In the Bible it's written, "And be thankful." That's what we need to be when we receive our gifts, especially those little gifts.

Let us pray.

Dear God: Remind us to be thankful for even the little gifts. Amen.

No. 50

How Many Days to Go?

Do you mind if I read the newspaper while I talk to you this morning? I have one in my brown bag. All I want to read is the right-hand corner of the front page.

Why only the right-hand corner? Well, let me tell you what is in that corner, and then you'll know. There is a little box with a number in it. For those of you who have noticed it, you know it tells how many more shopping days we have until Christmas.

When I was about your age, every day during Advent (that's the season before Christmas) I would look to see what this number was. I looked at it even before I looked at the "funnies." And I still do this—even before I read my favorite comic strips and the sports page.

Let me tell you something else I used to do. When the family had read the paper, I would tear out that little reminder and keep it in my pocket all day long, looking at it often. It was my way of saying, "I just can't wait!" Oh, I guess I could have looked at the calendar in the kitchen, but that would have been too much out of my way. Besides, I would have had to count each day remaining, and that was too much work. Instead, I carried the number with me.

Here, let's check on this number for today. As I
unfold this paper, our eyes can't keep from looking
toward the right-hand corner. SEVENTEEN.

So, we have seventeen days to go before we
share our gifts of love. But why do we have to wait
seventeen days before we do this?

Don't misunderstand my question. I'm not
suggesting that you can give and receive your
Christmas gifts today. Your parents wouldn't be very
happy with me if I told you that.

As we look at this number, however, we keep
saying to ourselves, "I just can't wait!" Again I say,
we don't have to! No, I'm not talking about the
purchased gifts we give at Christmastime. I'm talking
about the love that can't wait. Love isn't to be given
to those people nearest and dearest to us just on a
special holiday, such as on Christmas or even
Valentine's Day. It's something we need to give every
day of the year.

This is what God does! It's true that love came
down at Christmastime long ago and that each
Christmas that love makes us happy as we celebrate
the birth of Jesus. In the Bible we read, "For God so
loved the world. . . ." Because of Jesus we know this
is true, for every day of the year.

The gift of love should be given 365 days a
year—all year long. So, why wait? Give it today,
tomorrow, every day, as well as on Christmas.

Let us pray.
Dear God: May we give gifts of love every day.
Amen.

No. 51

What's It All About?

It's almost Christmas. Only a few days to go. What's it all about?

Right. It's all about the birth of Jesus. That's why I have my brown bag turned upside down this morning. Let me lift it, and you will see. A crèche.

Is that a new word for you? Say it with me. Crèche. It's a French word for a manger scene, showing Mary and Joseph, the wise men, the shepherds and their sheep, all grouped around Jesus, with the star shining down on them.

This crèche was made at our Advent workshop a few weeks ago. Maybe you and your parents made one. Although this particular crèche doesn't have the wise men or the shepherds or the sheep or the star, these could be added. It just shows the manger area, with Jesus' parents standing by the crib in which Jesus lies. Notice what they are made of—clothespins.

I've seen crèches made out of many things: glass, stone, cornhusks, metal, plastic, clay, and bottles covered with cloth. I've even seen a real live manger scene where someone was Mary and another person was Joseph, while others were the wise men and shepherds. Yes, they had real animals—cows, donkeys, sheep—but they couldn't get a camel. In the manger was a real baby (very warmly wrapped).

I read somewhere that this is how the crèche idea was first started. It was Francis of Assisi (a very great man in the church who lived many hundreds of years ago) who first used real people and real animals for a manger scene. This scene was in front of the village church, and when the people came to the church that Christmas night the persons in the crèche began singing a Christmas carol Saint Francis had written. What a wonderful idea!

But remember, it's all to remind us of the birth of Jesus. You see, Jesus wasn't born in a hospital or a hotel or at home. His father and mother were away from their home when he was born. They wanted to stay in the inn, which was much like a hotel, but they were told there was "no vacancy"— all the rooms were filled. Instead, the innkeeper let them stay where the cows and donkeys and other animals were bedded down. That is where Jesus was born on that night long ago in the city of Bethlehem. And he was carefully wrapped in a piece of cloth and laid in the manger, the place where they put the straw and hay for the animals to eat. Then, the shepherds came, and later the wise men, with the star which told of his birth shining down on them.

Can't you just picture that in your mind? And what a lovely picture it is! That's why we have the crèche, to help us remember what happened there in that stable.

What's it all about? It's about the birth of Jesus. And even more than this—important as this is to us—it's about God's love becoming very real to us through this Jesus. "In this the love of God was made manifest among us" is the way the Bible says it.

On this Christmas, let's remember the birth of Jesus and tell of God's love for us all.

Let us pray.
Dear God: Thank you for Jesus and the love he brought to us. Amen.

DENNIS the MENACE

"AND HELP ME TO BE A BETTER KID. AMEN."

"NOW THAT WE'RE ALONE.."

No. 52

Now That We're Alone

When you say your prayers, are you usually
alone—just you and God?

That's the way I like to pray most of the time.
Oh, there are times when it is good to pray with
others or to pray for others when they are there. On
Sunday morning we do both. We have the time of
silent prayers when each of us can talk with God, but
we also have the time when we pray out loud with
others or when I pray to God for us.

I hope that when I pray in church each person
will take my words, or the printed prayers in the
bulletin, and make them a personal prayer. That is the
way prayer should always be—a personal conversation
between each of us and God.

How many of you like to read "Dennis the
Menace" in the daily newspaper? I always check out
what Dennis is up to, for he is one of my favorites.
Several days ago I saw a "Dennis the Menace" that I
would like to share with you this morning. To help
you see this little cartoon better, I've had it enlarged
to three feet by two feet. Here, let me thumbtack this
big picture on the bulletin board I have on this easel
so you can see it.

In the first part of the drawing, Dennis' mother is
listening as he says his prayers while kneeling beside
his bed. He says, "And help me to be a better kid.
Amen." Then, in the second half of the drawing, his

mother has gone, and Dennis says, "Now that we're ALONE."

I understand how Dennis felt. There are times when I don't want anyone to hear what I have to tell God. When I've done something I shouldn't have done and I'm very ashamed of myself, it is then that I want to say to God, "Now that we're ALONE."

And God listens! No matter what we've done, God listens very carefully to what we say. We can talk with God about anything, and God understands us and loves us in spite of what we have done wrong. In fact, God does more than just listen to our prayers, God also seeks to help us be better.

This is really important to remember. Tonight, either before you crawl into bed or after you've crawled between the covers, say to God, "Now that we're ALONE." Then tell God how you feel, how you need help, and what you have done that is wrong. God will hear you and help you. And tell God how thankful you are.

By the way, you don't have to limit yourself just to telling God what you've done wrong or how much help you need to be good. You can talk to God about anything you want to.

Yes, God awaits that time when we're alone to talk about anything and everything.

Let us pray.
Dear God: Thank you for listening to us and understanding us. Amen.